Pope Francis
IN HIS OWN WORDS

Pope Francis
IN HIS OWN WORDS

edited by
Julie Schwietert Collazo
and Lisa Rogak

New World Library
Novato, California

New World Library
14 Pamaron Way
Novato, California 94949

Text design by Tona Pearce Myers

Quotations from Spanish-language sources translated by Julie Schwietert Collazo and Francisco Collazo

Library of Congress Cataloging-in-Publication Data is available.

First printing, May 2013
ISBN 978-1-60868-248-5
Printed in the USA on 100% postconsumer-waste recycled paper

New World Library is proud to be a Gold Certified Environmentally Responsible Publisher. Publisher certification awarded by Green Press Initiative. www.greenpressinitiative.org

10 9 8 7 6 5 4 3 2 1

Contents

Introduction

"I'll just go with the guys on the bus."

The newly elected Pope Francis, speaking to his limo driver
and security detail after his initial introduction to crowds in Rome

With the election of Argentina's Cardinal Jorge Mario Bergoglio as the new pope of the Catholic Church in March 2013, attention has turned worldwide toward not only what he will do as pope but how he has lived — and preached — in the past. So far, it's very clear that, compared to other popes, he has led a humble and unconventional life. For instance, as a cardinal, instead of asking to be addressed as Your Eminence, he preferred to simply be called Father Jorge.

Some of the first photos to be published after he was introduced to happy throngs of worshippers in St. Peter's

Square reveal that humility and the desire to serve the poor run deep in his blood. One photo showed him kneeling to wash a woman's feet, while news reports told of his performing the same service for AIDS patients. It's hard to imagine his predecessor at the Vatican doing likewise.

It's clear that his humility and desire to meet with the people on their level — whether they're Catholics or not — has already won him huge numbers of fans. He cracks jokes, doesn't hesitate to challenge his country's leaders on their inequities, and pushes away chauffeurs and luxury transport in order to press the flesh with commoners. And numerous news stories have shown that he offers great compassion toward those who have long been ostracized by churches of all stripes.

At the same time, he shows that he's a real person, with human desires that he indulges wholeheartedly (well, at least a few…). After all, when was the last time you heard of a pope who admitted to loving tango and who had pledged his undying loyalty to one Buenos Aires soccer club since childhood?

He also walks his talk, which instantly won him respect and admiration around the world. During his tenure as a cardinal in Buenos Aires, Bergoglio refused to live in the luxury accommodations in the palace that previous cardinals called home. Instead, he rented a spartan one-bedroom apartment where he cooked his own simple dinners, took the bus to work, and persuaded the diocese to allow a group of poor missionaries to live in the official residence.

❧

The Catholic Church essentially crossed three first-evers off the list in mid-March 2013 when the Conclave chose Jorge Mario Bergoglio to be the new pontiff.

First of all, he is the first Jesuit ever elected to the office. The Jesuit order has a reputation as one of the most rebellious in Catholicism — often standing in direct conflict with traditional Church doctrine — while also being known for its intellectual rigor.

Second, he is the first pope to come from the Americas, and more specifically, the first to come from Latin America, the region that holds the largest percentage of the worldwide Catholic population, at almost 40 percent.

Third, he is the first pontiff to select the name Francis, in homage to St. Francis of Assisi, an Italian who devoted his life to the poor and formed the religious order of the Franciscans.

To Catholics, accustomed to the stern, authoritarian approach of Pope Benedict XVI, the Conclave's election of Jorge Mario Bergoglio is heartwarming and joyous, harkening back to the more personable days of Pope John Paul II. And since the Pope is essentially a world leader, on the same footing with presidents and premiers, there's no doubt that other world leaders are already lining up for an audience with him.

In just a short time, Pope Francis has made an indelible impact on Catholics, making them feel optimistic about their faith and, in turn, their lives.

For Catholics and others who are curious about the new Pope, the best way to learn more about him is through his own writings — he has written a number of books and countless letters and sermons — and past interviews. *Pope Francis in His Own Words* will allow readers to do just that, with his views and thoughts condensed into neatly concise, bite-sized bits so everyone — Catholic or not — can immediately learn more about "Father Jorge."

Pope Francis
IN HIS OWN WORDS

On Age and Aging

Old age, they say, is the seat of wisdom. The old ones have the wisdom that they have earned from walking through life, like old Simeon and Anna at the temple, whose wisdom allowed them to recognize Jesus. Let us give with wisdom to the youth: like good wine that improves with age, let us give the youth the wisdom of our lives.

Address to Cardinals, 15 March 2013

꤮

The old person is the transmitter of history, he who brings us memories, the memory of our people, of our country, of our family, culture, and religion.... He has lived a long time, and even if he's done so as a fool, he deserves serious consideration.

Sobre el Cielo y la Tierra, 2010

The bitterness of the old person is worse than any other because it is without return.

Sobre el Cielo y la Tierra, 2010

On Argentina

Is it true that Argentinians don't want to dialogue? I wouldn't put it that way. Rather, I think we've become victims of attitudes that don't permit us to dialogue: arrogance, the inability to listen, an exasperation with language...and so many others.

Sobre el Cielo y la Tierra, 2010

Our painful political history has all too often courted silence. The use of euphemisms has often anesthetized us.

Homily, Easter 2008

Argentina has arrived at a moment of critical decision making...the decision to continue as a country, to learn from its painful experiences of the past and initiate a new path, or to drown in misery, chaos, the loss of values, and decomposition as a society.

Annual Message to Educational Communities, Easter 2002

⌒

I dare to say it still: we Argentinians have a long history of mutual intolerance.

Homily, Easter 2005

⌒

We live in the most unequal part of the world, which has grown the most, yet reduced misery the least. The unjust distribution of goods persists, creating a situation of social sin that cries out to heaven and limits the possibilities of a fuller life for so many of our brothers.

Address, CELAM conference, 21 May 2007

On Argentina's Dirty War

In the Church, there were Christians from [all] camps: Christians who died as guerrillas, Christians who helped save people, and Christian oppressors who believed they were saving the homeland.

Sobre el Cielo y la Tierra, 2010

❧

We believe that the steps taken by the justice system in clarifying these events must serve to renew the efforts of all citizens toward reconciliation, and are a call to distance ourselves not only from impunity but from hatred and rancor as well. [Any Catholic who participated did so] on his own responsibility, erring and sinning gravely against God, against mankind, and against his own conscience.

Interpress Service, 11 October 2007

❧

The horrors committed under the military governments were revealed only drip by drip, but for me they are still one of the worst blights on this country.

Sobre el Cielo y la Tierra, 2010

On Argentina's Leaders

Rather than preventing [them], it seems [the Argentinian government has] opted for making inequalities even greater.

Guardian, 13 March 2013

On Art and Artists

Artists know well that beauty isn't solely consoling, but that it can also be disturbing. The grand masters have known how to present with beauty those realities of the human condition that are most tragic and painful.

Speech, ADEPA, 6 April 2006

Argentina has given the world many writers and artists of quality...in every genre, from the most traditional to those that express the views of the youngest generations — all saying something about who we are and who we want to be!

Annual Message to Educational Communities, Easter 2006

His favorite painting:
The White Crucifixion by Marc Chagall

El Jesuita, 2010

On Asking Catholics for Their Prayers

I would like to give you a blessing, but first I want to ask you for a favor. Before the bishop blesses the people, I ask that you pray to the Lord so that He blesses me.

First blessing as Pope, 13 March 2013

On Aspirations

No one can grow if he does not accept his smallness.

Homily, 25 May 2006

On Assisted Suicide

In Argentina there is clandestine euthanasia. Social services pay up to a certain point; if you pass it, "die, you are very old." Today, elderly people are discarded when, in reality, they are the seat of wisdom of the society. The right to life means allowing people to live and not killing, allowing them to grow, to eat, to be educated, to be healed, and to be permitted to die with dignity.

LifeSiteNews.com, 5 October 2007

❧

[Euthanasia is] a culture of discarding the elderly.

Speech, Aparecida Document, 2 October 2007

On Atheists

I don't say that [the atheist's] life is condemned [to Hell], because I am convinced I don't have the right to pass judgment about the moral uprightness of that person.

Sobre el Cielo y la Tierra, 2010

❧

Not everyone present belongs to the Catholic faith, and others do not believe. I respect the conscience of each one of you, knowing that each one of you is a child of God. May God bless you.

Vatican press conference, 16 March 2013

❧

[I] know more agnostics than atheists; the first is more undecided, the second, more convinced.

Sobre el Cielo y la Tierra, 2010

On Baptizing the Children of Single Parents

The child has absolutely no responsibility for the state of his parents' marriage. And often a baptism can be a new start for the parents as well.

30 Giorni, August 2009

～

In our ecclesiastical region, there are priests who don't baptize the children of single mothers because they weren't conceived in the sanctity of marriage. These are today's hypocrites: those who clericalize the Church, those who separate the people of God from salvation. And this poor girl who, rather than returning the child to sender, had the courage to carry it into the world, must wander from parish to parish until her child can be baptized!

New York Daily News, 14 March 2013

On Beauty

Few things are more moving than the human need for beauty that all hearts have.

Speech, ADEPA, 6 April 2006

～

Because it is human, sometimes beauty is tragic, surprising, moving; on some occasions, it compels us to think about what we do not want or it shows us the error of our ways.

Speech, ADEPA, 6 April 2006

On Being Chosen as Pope

As you know, the duty of the Conclave is to give Rome a bishop. It seems that my brother cardinals went almost to the end of the world. But here we are.

First blessing as Pope, 13 March 2013

❧

May God forgive you.

First dinner with cardinals after election as Pope, 13 March 2013

On Being Right... and Wrong

I don't have all the answers. Nor do I have all the questions.... I confess that, in general, because of my temperament, the first response that occurs to me is the wrong one.... It's curious, but that's the way it is with me.

El Jesuita, 2010

On Birth Control

[Anti-condom zealots want to] stick the whole world inside a condom.

Sobre el Cielo y la Tierra, 2010

On Bridezilla Weddings

In some churches — and I don't know how to remedy this, honestly — there is a fierce competition between bridesmaids and brides. These women aren't observing a religious act; they're just showing off. And this weighs on my conscience; as priest, I am permitting this and I haven't found a way to put a stop to it.

Sobre el Cielo y la Tierra, 2010

On Buenos Aires

Distracted city, dispersed city, egotistical city: cry. You need to be purified by your tears....Let this scatter-brained, superficial city be purified by its grief.

Homily, 30 December 2005

For many, Buenos Aires is a factory of slaves...a meat grinder which destroys their lives, breaks their will, and deprives them of freedom.

Vatican Insider, 15 December 2011

≈

After 52 commuters died when a train crashed into buffers at a railway station in Buenos Aires:
This city does not know how to weep. All is fixed with anesthetics...virtually all of them were earning their daily bread. With dignity! Father, let us not get used to the idea that to earn your daily bread you must travel like cattle.

Homily, 23 March 2012

≈

At school they taught us slavery has been abolished, but do you know what? It was a fairy tale! Because in Buenos Aires, slavery has not been abolished; in this city it is still common in various forms; in this city workers are exploited in clandestine workshops and, if they are immigrants, they prevent them from leaving; and in this city there are children who have been living on the streets for years.... In this city women are kidnapped and are submitted to the use and abuse of their bodies, destroying their dignity. There are men here who abuse and make money from human flesh.... Dogs are treated better than these slaves of ours!

Homily, 23 September 2011

How lovely it is to walk this way, slowly, feeling the presence of others, singing, looking forward, looking at the sky, praying for those who aren't with us in Buenos Aires!

Homily, 24 May 2008

When I pray for the city of Buenos Aires, I give thanks for the fact that it was the city where I was born.

Address to the First Congress of Regional Urban Parishes,
25 August 2011

On Cardinals

The cardinalate is a service; it is not an award to be bragged about.

Vatican Insider, 24 February 2012

✎

Cardinals are not NGO representatives, but servants of the Lord, inspired by the Holy Spirit, which is the one [that] is really able to differentiate charismas, unifying them in the Church. A cardinal must be able to differentiate between charismas and at the same time look toward unity, aware that the creator of difference and unity is the Holy Spirit itself. Cardinals who do not enter this frame of mind, in my view, are not cardinals in the way Benedict XVI would like them to be.

Vatican Insider, 24 February 2012

On Catechists

I hope that there is no room among you for apostolic mummies... please, no! Go to a museum — mummies look better there.

Address at Archdiocese Meeting, 12 March 2005

On Catholic Life

When one does not walk, one halts. When one does not build on stone, what happens? That happens which happens to children on the beach when they make sand castles: it all comes down; it is without substance.

Homily, first papal Mass, 14 March 2013

∽

To walk, to build, to confess. But the matter is not so easy, because in walking, in building, in confessing, at times there are shocks, there are movements that are not properly movements of the journey: they are movements that set us back.

Homily, first papal Mass, 14 March 2013

On Celibacy in Priests

Yes, hypothetically, western Catholicism could revise the theme of celibacy.... But for the moment, I am in favor of maintaining celibacy, with the pros and the cons it has, because we have ten centuries of more good experiences than bad ones.

Sobre el Cielo y la Tierra, 2010

On Character Flaws

Isn't it fickle, mediocre vanity that makes us build walls, whether they are walls of riches or power, or violence and impunity?

Homily, 25 May 2011

◦❧◦

It astonished and perplexed me when I asked an acquaintance how he was doing and he responded, "Bad, but used to it."

Homily, 22 February 2012

On Child Labor

The promotion and strengthening of work for adults will make it possible to avoid [the phenomenon] of child labor. It's very difficult for a child to go out and look for work if his parents have meaningful work that allows them to provide for their family's needs.

Letter for the Youth, 1 October 2005

◦❧◦

On Children

What world are we leaving our children? Maybe it would be better to ask, "What children are we giving this world?"

Homily, 1 September 1999

We have, in our hands, the responsibility and also the possibility of making this world much better for our children.

Homily, Easter 2005

We should be cognizant of the emergency facing our children and our young people.

Letter for the Youth, 1 October 2005

So many children don't know how to pray!

Homily, Ash Wednesday 2004

Children are mistreated, and are not educated or fed. Many are made into prostitutes and exploited. And this happens here in Buenos Aires, in the great city of the south. Child prostitution is offered in some five-star hotels: it is included in the entertainment menu, under the heading "Other."

Speech, 2 October 2007

On Choices

Each day, we all face the choice to be Good Samaritans or to be indifferent travelers passing by.

Homily, 25 May 2003

On Choosing the Name Francis

The man of the poor. The man of peace. The man who loved and cared for creation — and in this moment we don't have such a great relationship with the creator. The man who gives us this spirit of peace, the poor man who wanted a poor church.

Vatican press conference, 16 March 2013

Francis is also the man of peace. That is how the name came into my heart: Francis of Assisi. For me, he is the man of poverty, the man of peace, the man who loves and protects creation.

Vatican press conference, 16 March 2013

❧

[Francis of Assisi] brought to Christianity an idea of poverty against the luxury, pride, [and] vanity of the civil and ecclesiastical powers of the time. He changed history.

Sobre el Cielo y la Tierra, 2010

On the Christian Life

The Christian truth is attractive and persuasive because it responds to the deep needs of human existence, convincingly announcing that Christ is the only Savior of the whole person and of all persons. This announcement is as valid today as it was at the beginning of Christianity, when there was a great missionary expansion of the Gospel.

Address to Cardinals, 15 March 2013

❧

[Living] the Christian life [means] giving witness with joy, just as Jesus did.

El Jesuita, 2010

❧

The Christian life is always a walk in the presence of God, but it is not exempt from struggles and trials.

Homily, 11 March 2006

❧

In the life of every Christian ... there will be the experience of the desert, of interior purification, of the dark night.

Homily, 11 March 2006

On Christmas

What is the spirit of Christmas? Over the years the world of culture has tried to express it in a thousand ways and has managed to take us closer to the meaning of the Christmas spirit. How many Christmas stories bring us closer to this?

La Nación, 23 December 2011

On the Church

We have to avoid the spiritual sickness of a self-referential Church. It's true that when we stray from its path, as can happen to any man or woman, accidents can happen. But if the Church stays enclosed within itself, self-referential, it will grow old. And between a Church that accidentally strays off its path and one that is sick because of self-reference, I have no doubt: I prefer the former.

El Jesuita, 2010

༄

If, throughout history, the Church has changed so much, I do not see why we should not adapt it to the culture of [our] time.

Sobre el Cielo y la Tierra, 2010

༄

The Church is Mother and talks to the people as a mother talks to her child, with that confidence that the child already knows that everything he is being taught is for his good, because he knows he is loved.

Speech, "The Sunday Homily in Latin America," 19 January 2005

The Church was, is, and will continue to be persecuted.

Homily, 23 April 2007

How I would love a Church that is poor and for the poor.

Vatican press conference, 16 March 2013

I must not be scandalized by the fact that the Church is my mother: I must look at its sins and shortcomings as I would look at my mother's sins and shortcomings. And when I think of her, I remember the good and beautiful things she has achieved, more than her weaknesses and defects. A mother defends herself with a heart filled with love before doing so with words. I wonder whether there is any love for the Church in the hearts of those who pay so much attention to the scandals.

America magazine, 15 March 2013

On the Church in Buenos Aires

Instead of just being a Church that welcomes and receives, we try to be a Church that comes out of itself and goes to the men and women who do not participate in parish life, do not know much about it and are indifferent toward it. We organize missions in public squares where many people usually gather: we pray, we celebrate Mass, and we offer baptism, which we administer after a brief preparation.

Vatican Insider, 24 February 2013

On Church Politics

The Pope [Benedict XVI]...talked about James and John and the tensions between the first followers of Jesus on who should be first. This shows us that certain attitudes and arguments have existed in the Church since the beginning.

Vatican Insider, 24 February 2012

There are sectors within the religions that are so prescriptive that they forget the human side.

Sobre el Cielo y la Tierra, 2010

❧

There have been corrupt periods. There were very difficult periods, but the religion revived itself.

Sobre el Cielo y la Tierra, 2010

On the Church's Emphasis on Suffering

It is true that at one time, [the Church] really emphasized the matter of suffering. The exaltation of suffering in the Church depends a great deal on the era and the culture [in question].

El Jesuita, 2010

On Cities

Every big city has many riches, many possibilities, but also many dangers.

Homily, 12 March 2005

❧

The city is also a mother.

Homily, 30 December 2005

On Citizenship

Political society will only endure if the satisfaction of common human needs is our vocation. This is the role of the citizen.

Homily, 25 May 1999

꙳

We are historical people. We live in time and space. Every generation needs the ones before it and owes those who follow. And this, in great measure, is what it means to be a nation: to understand ourselves as continuing the work of other men and women who have already done their part.

Annual Message to Educational Communities, Easter 2002

꙳

We don't have to expect everything from those who govern us; that would be juvenile.

Homily, 25 May 2003

꙳

People are historical subjects, which is to say, citizens and members of the *pueblo* [nation]. The state and society should generate the social conditions that promote and act as guardian of their rights and allow them to be builders of their own destiny.

Speech, Archdiocesan Social Pastoral Conference, 16 October 2010

On Civilization

It is possible to build a new civilization centered on love and life.

Homily, 25 September 2004

On the Conclave

The period of the Conclave was full of meaning, not only for the College of Cardinals, but also for all the faithful. In these days we felt, almost tangibly, the affection and solidarity of the universal Church, as well as the attention of many people who, although they do not share our faith, look to the Church and the Holy See with respect and admiration.

Address to Cardinals, 15 March 2013

On Conversation

Would it be possible for us to be more attentive to what we say to others and what we don't say?

Annual Message to Educational Communities, Easter 2002

❧

In order to have dialogue, you have to know how to lower your defenses, open the doors of your home, and offer human warmth.

Sobre el Cielo y la Tierra, 2010

❧

True growth in human consciousness cannot be founded on anything other than the practice of dialogue and love.

Annual Message to Educational Communities, Easter 2002

On Creativity

The challenge of creative beings is to be suspicious of every discourse, thought, affirmation, or proposal that presents itself as "the only possible path." There are always others. There is always another possibility.

Annual Message to Educational Communities, 9 April 2003

❧

If to build something we always undo and step on what others have done before us, how can we create something solid?

Annual Message to Educational Communities, 9 April 2003

On Death

Death is on my mind every day.

El Jesuita, 2010

On the Death of Argentinian President Néstor Kirchner

And we are here today to pray for a man named Néstor, who was received by the hands of God and who, in his moment, was anointed by his people [to lead].

Homily, 27 October 2010

On the Death Penalty

Before, it was one of those punishments that Christianity accepted. But today moral conscience has become more refined and the catechism says it would be better if [capital punishment] didn't exist.

Sobre el Cielo y la Tierra, 2010

On Democracy

Of course, participating in political life is a way of honoring democracy.

Sobre el Cielo y la Tierra, 2010

On the Devil

Theologically speaking, the Devil is a being who chose not to accept God's plan.

Sobre el Cielo y la Tierra, 2010

જ્જ

Whoever does not pray to God, prays to the Devil.

First homily as Pope, 15 March 2013

જ્જ

In my own experience, I feel [the presence of] the Devil every time I'm tempted to do something that isn't what God asked of me.

Sobre el Cielo y la Tierra, 2010

On Dignity

There is not a single violation of the dignity of a woman or man that can be justified in the name of any other thing or idea. Not a single one.

Annual Message to Educational Communities, 18 April 2007

⁓

When a person or a people sells its dignity or bargains it…everything else loses consistency and ceases to have worth.

Homily, 7 August 2007

On Doubt

The greatest leaders in God's tribe have been those men who have left room for doubt.

Sobre el Cielo y la Tierra, 2010

On Drugs

Alcohol and drugs are an easy shortcut

Guardian, 14 March 2013

On Education

Education is the genuine expression of social love.

Annual Message to Educational Communities, 27 April 2006

On Elitism

The impatience of the illustrious elites doesn't understand the laborious, daily march of the people, nor the message of the wise man.

Homily, 25 May 2004

On Evangelism

We have to go out and talk to people in the city who we've seen on their balconies. We have to come out of our shell and tell them that Jesus lives…to say it with joy…even though it seems a little crazy sometimes.

Homily, 11 March 2000

On Exclusivity

Sometimes, I ask myself if we, the Church, are complicit with a culture of exclusion, one in which there is no longer space for the old person, for the child, where there is no time to stop on the side of the road like the Good Samaritan.

Homily, 12 March 2005

On Faith

People ask why we spend our time touching a statue when we could be out looking for work. We do it because faith will see us through. We do it because faith endures. We do it because faith is all we have at a time like this.

Washington Post, 8 August 2003

❧

Benedict XVI has insisted on the renewal of faith being a priority and presents faith as a gift that must be passed on, a gift to be offered to others and to be shared as a gratuitous act. It is not a possession, but a mission.

Vatican Insider, 24 February 2012

On Family

The family is the natural center of human life.

Parish and Family, 18 January 2007

❧

The Church tries to demonstrate the modern mentality that the family founded on marriage has two essential values for all societies and all cultures: stability and fecundity.

Parish and Family, 18 January 2007

❧

Roles of fatherhood, motherhood, being a son or daughter, and brother or sister, are the basis of any society, and without them every society would lose consistency and turn toward anarchy.

Parish and Family, 18 January 2007

On Foreign Business

Money also has a homeland, and he who exploits an industry in a country and takes the money to another country to store it is sinning, because he is not honoring with that money that country that enriched him.

Sobre el Cielo y la Tierra, 2010

On Forgiveness

We ask for the grace of never tiring of asking for forgiveness, for He never tires of forgiving.

Homily, 17 March 2013

❧

If the Lord did not forgive everything, the world would not exist.

Homily, 17 March 2013

On Fragility

I invite you to recognize the treasure hidden in your fragility.

Homily, 21 August 2003

❧

God, when He looks at our fragility, invites us to tend to it not with fear, but with audacity.

Homily, 8 April 2004

On Freedom

The blindness of spirit prevents us from being free.

Homily, 25 May 2004

❧

This is the struggle of every person: be free or be a slave.

Homily, 4 September 2003

On Giving Money to Beggars

Sometimes I ask someone who is making confession if they give alms to beggars. When they tell me, "Yes," I ask, "And do you look in the eyes of the person to whom you are giving alms? Do you touch their hand?" And that's where they start to get tangled up, because many just throw the money and turn their heads.

Sobre el Cielo y la Tierra, 2010

On Globalization

To fight the effects of globalization that led to the closure of many factories and the consequences of misery and unemployment, you have to promote bottom-up economic growth with the creation of small and medium-sized companies. Outside help should not just come in the form of funds but should also reinforce a work culture and a political culture.

La Stampa, December 2001

❦

If we think of globalization like a billiard ball, it annihilates the rich virtues of each culture.

Sobre el Cielo y la Tierra, 2010

❦

Globalization, as an economic and social ideology, has negatively affected our poorest communities.

Address, CELAM conference, 21 May 2007

❦

Globalization as a unidirectional and uniform imposition of values, practices, and goods goes hand in hand with imitation and cultural, intellectual, and spiritual subordination.

Annual Message to Educational Communities, Easter 2002

❦

The kind of globalization that makes things uniform is essentially imperialist. At the end it becomes a way of enslaving people.

Sobre el Cielo y la Tierra, 2010

Globalization has signified an accelerated deterioration of cultural roots, what with the invasion of other cultural tendencies, be they in music, fast-food businesses, malls, means of communication, etc.

Address, CELAM conference, 21 May 2007

From Bangkok to São Paulo, from Buenos Aires to Los Angeles or Sydney, many young people are listening to the same music; kids see the same cartoons; families dress, eat, and have fun in the same stores. Nonetheless, this globalization is an ambiguous reality.

Annual Message to Educational Communities, Easter 2002

At no other moment in history has humanity had the possibility, as it does now, of building a plural, unified world community.

Annual Message to Educational Communities, Easter 2002

On God

What God cares about most is that we are His friends.

Homily, 17 April 2003

We can say, without being irreverent: there isn't anyone more "inefficient" than God.

Annual Message to Educational Communities, Easter 2004

God is not like the idols, who have ears but don't listen. He's not like the powerful, who listen only to what they wish. He listens to everything...and He doesn't just listen; He loves to listen.

Homily, 7 August 2006

If we close the door of our heart in His face, God suffers. Even though He's used to it, He suffers. And we lose the opportunity for Him to make us happy.

Homily, 15 March 2008

∽⁐⊙

God isn't a kind of Andreani [UPS or FedEx], sending messages all the time.

Sobre el Cielo y la Tierra, 2010

On God's Gifts

When a man guards his gift and doesn't do his work, he doesn't fulfill his mandate and remains primitive; when he is overly enthusiastic about his work, he forgets his gift and creates a constructivist ethic: he believes everything is the fruit of his own hands and that there is no gift.

Sobre el Cielo y la Tierra, 2010

On God's Promises

He doesn't promise riches or power, but what He does promise is His care and the greatest security you can find: refuge in the name of God. He promises His intimacy, the warmth of the Father, [and] His embrace, full of tenderness and understanding.

Homily, 30 January 2005

On Good Intentions

Intention is not enough. It's not enough for our brothers and sisters who are most in need, the victims of injustice and exclusion, those whom "the interior of our hearts" doesn't help in their need. It's not even enough for ourselves.

Annual Message to Educational Communities, Easter 2004

On Gossip

What is gossip? It's a truth taken out of context.

El Jesuita, 2010

On Helping the Poor

The great danger — or the great temptation — of helping the poor lies in falling into the role of paternalistic protector, which ultimately doesn't let people grow.

Sobre el Cielo y la Tierra, 2010

On Himself

And, please, don't stop praying for me because, well, I need it.

Homily, 9 June 2007

❧

I don't like to talk about what I haven't seen or what I don't know.

Homily, 7 September 2008

On His Appointment as Pope

Before appearing on the balcony to greet people in St. Peter's Square:
I don't want to keep the people waiting.

Wall Street Journal, 13 March 2013

❧

First words to the crowd after his introduction as Pope:
Brothers and sisters, good evening.

Reuters, 13 March 2013

❧

And now, let us start this journey, Bishop and people, Bishop and people, this journey of the Church of Rome, which leads all the Churches in charity, a journey of fraternity, of love, of trust among us.

First blessing as Pope, 13 March 2013

On His Family History

[My parents] met in 1934 at Mass. They married the following year.

El Jesuita, 2010

On His Greatest Fear

It's true that the hedonistic, consumerist, narcissistic culture is infiltrating Catholicism. It's contaminating us.... In it rests the loss of the religious, which is what I fear most.

Sobre el Cielo y la Tierra, 2010

On His Humility

When offered a platform at his first appearance as Pope, which would place him above the cardinals around him:
I'll stay down here.

CNN, 14 March 2013

When offered a ride in a limo after becoming Pope:
I'll just go with the guys on the bus.

Associated Press, 13 March 2013

❧

When saying good-bye:
Pray for me.

Huffington Post, 14 March 2013

On His Mission as Pope

Repair my Church in ruins.

Catholic Online, 14 March 2013

On His Mother's Reaction
When He Joined the Priesthood

When I entered seminary, Mama didn't go with me; she didn't want to go. For years, she didn't accept my decision. We weren't fighting. It's just that I would go [visit her at] home, but she wouldn't come to the seminary. She was a religious woman, a practicing Catholic, but she thought that everything had happened too quickly. But I remember seeing her on her knees in front of me at the end of my ordination ceremony, asking for my blessing.

El Jesuita, 2010

On Homilies

A good Sunday homily should have the taste of that new wine, which renews the heart of he who is preaching as it renews that of his listeners.

Speech, "The Sunday Homily in Latin America," 19 January 2005

‿❧‿

The homily is not so much a moment of meditation and catechism as it is a living dialogue between God and his people.

Speech, "The Sunday Homily in Latin America," 19 January 2005

On Homosexuality

The religious ministry sometimes calls attention to certain points of private or public life because it is the guide of its parishioners. What it does *not* have the right to do is force a [specific kind of] private life on anyone. If God,

in His creation, ran the risk of making us free, who am I
to meddle?

Sobre el Cielo y la Tierra, 2010

On Hope

Hope is the capacity to weigh everything and keep the
best of each thing, to discern.

Annual Message to Educational Communities, Easter 2000

∽

Where there is hope, there is happiness.

Homily, 10 April 2002

On Human Beings

There are two types of men: those who take care of the
pain and those who pass by.

Homily, 25 May 2003

On the Human Mystery

There's no guru here who can explain the human mystery to us, nobody who can say that this will be this way
and that we'll be okay.

Homily, 23 March 2012

On Human Trafficking and Slavery

No to slavery.... No to children, men, and women [treated as] discarded material. It's our flesh that's at stake here! It's our flesh that's being sold! The same flesh I have, that you have, is on sale! And you're not going to be moved for the flesh of your brother?!

Homily, 4 September 2009

On Humanity

Every human being is worthwhile.

Annual Message to Educational Communities, Easter 2002

༄

We human beings have a complex relationship with the world in which we live, precisely because of our dual condition of being children of the earth and children of God.

Annual Message to Educational Communities, 18 April 2007

On Hypocrites in the Church

We should commit ourselves to "Eucharistic coherence"; that is, we should be conscious that people cannot receive Holy Communion and at the same time act or speak against the commandments, in particular when abortions, euthanasia, and other serious crimes against life and family are facilitated. This responsibility applies particularly to legislators, governors, and health professionals.

Speech, Aparecida Document, 2 October 2007

On Idolatry

The most dangerous idol is our own selves when we want to occupy the place of God.

Homily, 11 September 2004

On Images and Information

When images and information have as their sole objective the intent of provoking consumption or manipulating people ... we find ourselves in front of an assault, an act of violence, a kidnapping.

Homily, 10 October 2002

On Immigrants and Immigration

It seems that nobody here hates the immigrant. But subtle xenophobia exists....If we are sincere, we have to recognize that among us there is a subtle form of xenophobia, which is exploitation of the immigrant.

Homily, 7 September 2008

❧

I confess to you: when I meditate on [xenophobia in Argentina], I pardon [the xenophobes], but I cry. I cry out of impotence. What is happening to my people, who once had their arms open to receive so many immigrants? What is happening to my people?

Homily, 7 September 2008

On Indifference

Indifference is dangerous, whether innocent or not.

Homily, 25 May 2003

❧

Those of us who do nothing...are complicit in exploitation, slavery [and other social ills.] We are complicit through our silence, through our inaction, through our apathy.

Homily, 7 September 2008

❧

We do not have the right to be indifferent or to look the other way.

Homily, 25 May 2003

On Inequality

You have to become indignant against the injustice that not everyone has bread and work. In this world many people look out for themselves. And how curious it is that those who look out for themselves and not for the common good are usually the ones who go around cursing, who curse other people and things.

Speech, August 2012

On Injustice

Perhaps the worst injustice of the present time is the triumph of bitterness.

Annual Message to Educational Communities, 29 March 2000

In the face of grave forms of social and economic injustice, of political corruption, of ethnic cleansing, of demographic extermination, and destruction of the environment...surges the need for a radical personal and social renewal that is capable of ensuring justice, solidarity, honesty, and transparency.

Homily, 25 September 2004

⁓

It is not enough to avoid injustice if you're not promoting justice.

Homily, Easter 2005

On the Jesuits

[I] entered the Jesuit order because I was attracted by its...obedience and discipline. And by its focus on missionary work.

El Jesuita, 2010

On Jesus

Jesus took care of the details.

Homily, 17 April 2003

⁓

Jesus does not want us to be still, nor rushed; neither resting on our laurels, nor tense.

Homily, 24 May 2008

On Jewish–Catholic Relations

I sincerely hope I can contribute to the progress there has been in relations between Jews and Catholics since the Second Vatican Council in a spirit of renewed collaboration.

Letter to Rome's Chief Rabbi, 14 March 2013

On Latin America

The Church is very conscious of the fact that the cheapest thing in Latin America, the thing with the lowest price, is life.

Speech, 2 October 2007

❧

Latin America is experiencing, as the rest of the world is, a cultural transformation.

Homily, 19 January 2008

On Law

From the old "rules of courtesy," nearly nonexistent today, to legal obligations like paying taxes, all these are essential if we are to coexist and walk on a firmer path, to be more respectful and to create a sense of community.

Annual Message to Educational Communities, Easter 2006

On Leadership

Leadership is an art...that can be learned. It is also a science...that can be studied. It is a job...that demands dedication, effort, and tenacity. But above all, it is a mystery...that cannot always be explained with rational logic.

Speech, Archdiocesan Social Pastoral Conference, 16 October 2010

Every leader, to become a true leader, has to be, above all, a witness.

Speech, Archdiocesan Social Pastoral Conference, 16 October 2010

True leadership and the source of its authority is an existential experience.

Speech, Archdiocesan Social Pastoral Conference, 16 October 2010

On Life

Life is priceless.

Homily, 23 March 2012

On Life in the Twenty-First Century

It is the age of "weak thought."

Homily, 25 May 2004

⚬

Curiously, we have more information than ever, and yet we don't know what's going on.

Homily, 25 May 2004

On Listening

It's not always easy to listen. Sometimes it's more comfortable to play deaf, put on the Walkman and not listen to anyone. So easily we replace listening with email,

messaging, and "chat," and in this way we deprive ourselves...of faces, looks, and embraces.

El Verdadero Poder Es el Servicio, 2007

❧

How many problems would we avoid in life if we learned
to listen?

Homily, 5 October 2008

❧

Listening is also the capacity to share questions and the
search [for answers].

El Verdadero Poder Es el Servicio, 2007

On Love

To love is much more than feeling tenderness or a certain
emotion once in a while. It's a total challenge to creativity!

Annual Message to Educational Communities, 27 April 2006

❧

"But Father, I don't know how to love." No one knows how to love; we learn every day.

Homily, 21 April 2004

On Lying

Lies and thievery (the principal ingredients of corruption) are always evils that destroy the community.

Annual Message to Educational Communities, Easter 2002

On Marriage

When the husband or the wife gets accustomed to [the other's] love and to family, then they begin to stop valuing one another, to stop giving thanks and to stop taking care of what they have.

Homily, 17 February 2010

On Maturity

It seems to me that a meditation about maturity would do us all good.

Homily, Easter 2005

If maturity was only something that developed as part of our genetic code, then we really wouldn't have much to do.

Homily, Easter 2005

◦～

Maturity implies time.

Homily, Easter 2005

On the Media

Be assured that the Church, for her part, highly esteems your important work.... Your work calls for careful preparation, sensitivity, and experience, like so many other professions, but it also demands a particular concern for what is true, good, and beautiful. This is something which we have in common.

Vatican press conference, 16 March 2013

◦～

Journalists always present themselves before society as "searchers for the truth."

Speech, ADEPA, 6 April 2006

❧

When the news only makes us exclaim, "What an atrocity!" and immediately turn the page or change the channel, then we have destroyed [the sense of] proximity [to suffering], [and] we have widened even more the space that separates us.

Speech, ADEPA, 6 April 2006

❧

The media can, unfortunately, mirror society's worst aspects, or its most frivolous and narcissistic [qualities].

Homily, 10 October 2002

❧

The role of the mass media has expanded immensely in these years, so much so that they are an essential means of informing the world about the events of contemporary history. I would like, then, to thank you in a special way for the professional coverage which you provided during these days — you really worked, didn't you? — when the eyes of the whole world, and not just those of Catholics, were turned to the Eternal City.

Vatican press conference, 16 March 2013

On Mediocrity

Mediocrity is the best drug for enslaving the people.

Homily, 25 May 2004

On Memory

To make memories, to keep alive the memory of triumphs and failures, of moments of happiness and of suffering, is the only way to avoid being "children" in the worst sense of the word: immature, inexperienced, tremendously vulnerable.

Homily, Easter 2005

The manipulation of memory is never innocent; rather, it is dishonest.

Homily, Easter 2005

On Mercy

A little mercy makes the world less cold and more just.

Homily, 17 March 2013

❧

Only someone who has encountered mercy, who has been caressed by the tenderness of mercy, is happy and comfortable with the Lord. I beg the theologians who are present not to turn me in to the Sant'Uffizio or the Inquisition; however, forcing things a bit, I dare to say that the privileged locus of the encounter is the caress of the mercy of Jesus Christ on my sin.

National Catholic Reporter, 3 March 2013

❧

Mercy is the Lord's most powerful message. It's not easy to trust oneself to the mercy of God, because [His mercy] is an unfathomable abyss — but we must do it!

Homily, 17 March 2013

On the Mistreatment of Children

No one has the right to experiment with children and young people. They are the hope of the people, and we must take care of them by making responsible decisions.

Homily, 30 January 2005

❧

What is happening to our children? Or better put: what is happening with us, that we're incapable of taking charge of the situation of abandonment and loneliness in which our children find themselves?

Homily, Easter 2005

On Money

The measure of every human being is God, not money.

Annual Message to Educational Communities, 18 April 2007

On Morals

We speak of morals because it is easier. Furthermore — and this is bad taste — we deal with themes related to matrimonial morals and those tied to the sixth commandment because they seem more colorful. Thus we give a very sad image of the Church.

Vatican Insider, 15 December 2011

On Neoliberalism

The socioeconomic crisis and the resulting increase in poverty has its origins in policies inspired by forms of neoliberalism that consider profit and the laws of the market as absolute parameters above the dignity of people or of peoples.

Guardian, 14 March 2013

In the predominant neoliberal culture, the external, the immediate, the visible, the fast, the superficial: these occupy first place, and the real cedes ground to appearances.

Speech, CELAM conference, 21 May 2007

On Parenting

Without these three attitudes — tenderness, hope, and patience — it's impossible to respect life and the growth of the child who is waiting to be born.

Homily, 25 March 2004

〜

Only a mother and a father can say with joy, with pride, and with responsibility: we are going to be parents; we have conceived our child.

Homily, 7 August 2007

On Parties and Partying

The party occupies an important place. [It is] gratitude put in the form of joy, song, and dance. At a party, all the body's senses come into play, all in a setting of pleasure and joy.

Homily, 19 January 2008

On the Past

What was a sin and injustice also needs to be blessed with pardon, remorse, and reparation.

Homily, 9 June 2007

On Pedophile Priests

The idea that celibacy produces pedophiles can be forgotten. If a priest is a pedophile, he is so before he becomes a priest. But when this happens you must never look away.

You cannot be in a position of power and use it to destroy the life of another person.

Sobre el Cielo y la Tierra, 2010

∽⌇◦

I think that is the solution that was once proposed in the United States, of switching them to other parishes. That is stupid, because the priest continues to carry the problem in his backpack. The only answer to the problem is zero tolerance.

Sobre el Cielo y la Tierra, 2010

On Pessimism

Let us never give in to pessimism, to that bitterness that the Devil offers us every day. Do not give in to pessimism and discouragement.

Address to Cardinals, 15 March 2013

On Politicians

Sometimes they have to put out a fire, but the vocation of the politician is not that of a firefighter.

Speech, Archdiocesan Social Pastoral Conference, 2001

❧

Some people say to me, "But, Father, politicians aren't doing anything either!" But what are *you* doing? If you aren't doing anything, then scream [about yourself]!

Homily, 7 August 2008

On Politics

Politics is a noble activity. We should revalue it, practice it with vocation and a dedication that requires testimony, martyrdom — that is, to die for the common good.

Telegraph, 13 March 2013

❧

When asked why it took him four years to start seminary after deciding to join the priesthood:
It's true that I, like my entire family, was a practicing Catholic. But my head wasn't fixed solely on religious matters because I also had political preoccupations, although they didn't move beyond the intellectual plane. I read *Nuestra Palabra y Propositos*, a publication of the Communist Party, and I loved all the articles, which helped me in my political formation. But I was never a Communist.

El Jesuita, 2010

On Pope Benedict XVI

I think with great affection and deep gratitude of my venerable predecessor, Benedict XVI, who during these years of his pontificate has enriched and strengthened the Church with his teaching, his goodness, his guidance, his faith, his humility, and his gentleness, which will remain a spiritual heritage for all.

Address to Cardinals, 15 March 2013

It was [the Holy Spirit] who inspired the decision of Benedict XVI for the good of the Church.

Vatican press conference, 16 March 2013

On Possibilities

Human history, our history, the history of every one of us is never "finished"; it never runs out of possibilities. Rather, it is always opening to the new — to what, until now, we'd never even had in mind. To what seemed impossible.

Annual Message to Educational Communities, 9 April 2003

On Poverty

A community that stops kneeling before the rich, before success and prestige, and which is capable, instead, of washing the feet of the humble and those in need, will be more aligned with [God's] teaching than the winner-at-any-price ethic that we've learned — badly — in recent times.

Annual Message to Educational Communities, Easter 2002

❧

Is there anything more humiliating than being condemned [to an existence in which] you can't earn your daily bread?

Annual Message to Educational Communities, Easter 2002

On Power

If the most powerful used all his power to serve and to pardon, he who used his power for anything else would end up looking ridiculous.

Homily, 7 August 2005

❧

He who has a little more power has to serve a little more.

Homily, 7 August 2005

On Prayer

Let us always pray for us, one for the other; let us pray for the whole world, so that there may be a great fraternity.

First blessing as Pope, 13 March 2013

On the Priesthood

To be an open priest is to be capable of listening while remaining firm in one's convictions.

Letter to the Priests of the Archdiocese, 1 October 1999

༻༄

As pastors, it behooves each of us who offers Mass to renew each day, every Sunday, our passion for preparing the homily, ensuring, first of all, that knowledge of and love for the word of God are growing inside ourselves.

Speech, "The Sunday Homily in Latin America," 19 January 2005

On Priests Who Stray

If one of them comes to me and tells me he got a woman pregnant, I listen...[but] he must leave the ministry and take responsibility for his child....Just as the child has a right to have a mother, he also has the right to know his father's face. I commit to arranging the papers in Rome, but [the priest] must leave [the priesthood].

Sobre el Cielo y la Tierra, 2010

The double life doesn't do anyone good; I don't like it, it signifies a lie. If you can't overcome [your sexual needs], make a decision [priesthood or secular life].

Sobre el Cielo y la Tierra, 2010

On Prison Visits

It's horrific for me to go to a jail because what you see there is very hard. But I go anyway because God wants me to be face-to-face with the one who is most in need.

Sobre el Cielo y la Tierra, 2010

On Public Transportation

I almost always take [the subway] since it's fast, but I like the bus better because I can see the street.

El Jesuita, 2010

On the Relationship between Church and State

It isn't bad if religion dialogues with the political power; the problem is when it associates with it to do business under the table.

Sobre el Cielo y la Tierra, 2010

On Relativism

The modern city is relativist: everything is valid, and it's possible for us to give in to the temptation [of believing] that in order not to discriminate, in order to include everyone, that we have to occasionally "relativize" the truth. But this is not the case.

Speech, First Regional Conference of Urban Parishes, 25 August 2011

On Religious Diversity

The massive migratory movements of our world and the reality of religious diversity, especially that which originates in the East, present a delicate challenge to evangelization with respect to the encounter between different cultures and interreligious dialogue.

Homily, 25 September 2004

꧂

To recognize, accept, and live with all ways of thinking and being does not imply the renunciation of one's own beliefs.

Annual Message to Educational Communities, Easter 2006

On Religious Experiences

That is the religious experience: the astonishment of meeting someone who is waiting for you.

El Jesuita, 2010

On Religious Life

When we walk without the cross, when we build without the cross, and when we profess Christ without the cross, we are not disciples of the Lord: we are worldly; we are bishops, priests, cardinals, popes, but not disciples of the Lord.

Homily, first papal Mass, 14 March 2013

❧

Often, we feel fatigued and tired. Laziness tempts our spirits. We also look at all there is to do and the few we are.

Homily, Ash Wednesday 2004

❧

Jesus did not preach His own politics: He accompanied others. The conversions He inspired took place precisely because of His willingness to accompany, which makes us all brothers and children and not members of an NGO or proselytes of some multinational company.

Vatican Insider, 5 September 2012

On Religious Vocations

The religious vocation is a call from God to a heart that is ready, whether conscious of it or not.

El Jesuita, 2010

❧

The Church is in great need of moral theologians who can deepen Jesus's moral proposition [and] make it comprehensible to the contemporary man.

Homily, 25 September 2004

❧

Jesus teaches us another way. Go out! Go out! Share your testimony, go out and interact with your brothers, go out and share, go out and ask! Become the Word in body as well as in spirit.

New York Daily News, 14 March 2013

On Responsibility

We must stop hiding the pain of our losses and take responsibility for our crimes, our apathy, and our lies, because it is only through reparative reconciliation that we will be resuscitated, and, in the process, that we will lose fear of our own selves.

Homily, 25 May 2003

On the Role of Pope

Christ is the Church's pastor, but His presence in history passes through the freedom of human beings; from their midst one is chosen to serve as his vicar, the successor of the Apostle Peter.

Vatican press conference, 16 March 2013

On the Roman Curia

I see it as a body that gives service, a body that helps me and serves me.... The Roman Curia has its downsides, but I think that too much emphasis is placed on its negative aspects and not enough on the holiness of the numerous consecrated and laypeople who work in it.

Vatican Insider, 24 February 2012

On Rome

I hope that this journey of the Church that we begin today and which my cardinal vicar, who is here with me, will help me with, may be fruitful for the evangelization of this beautiful city.

Reuters, 13 March 2013

On Salvation

There is no middle ground: it's either light or dark, haughtiness or humility, the truth or the lie. We either open the door to Jesus, who comes to save us, or close it in [our belief in] self-sufficiency and the pride of self-salvation.

Homily, 25 December 2003

On Scandals in the Church

Look at the Church, holy and sinful as it is; look at certain shortcomings and sins, without losing sight of the holiness of so many men and women who work in the Church today.

Vatican Insider, 24 February 2012

On Schools

Our schools should be a space where our children and young people can have contact with the vitality of our history.

Annual Message to Educational Communities, 9 April 2003

The essential function of the school is to form free citizens with the capacity to defend their rights and comply with their obligations.

Letter for the Youth, 1 October 2005

∽⊙

If our schools are not a space where another humanity is being created, where another wisdom is taking root, where another society is being created, where hope and transcendence have a place, then we are losing out on making a unique contribution to this historical moment.

Annual Message to Educational Communities, Easter 2004

On Sectarianism

Sectarian attitudes in the social and political life of a country are terrible. They separate, divide, and drive us apart.

Guardian, 14 March 2013

On Self-Sufficiency

When someone is self-sufficient, when he has all the answers to all the questions, it's a sign that God is not with him.

Sobre el Cielo y la Tierra, 2010

On Service

Service is the rejection of indifference and utilitarian egotism. It is doing for others.

Homily, 25 May 2001

❧

Power is service, and service, to do it well, should attend to the smallest detail, the one that makes the other feel as if he has been well cared for [and] dignified.

Homily, 7 August 2005

❧

The person who is most high among us must be at the service of the others.

Homily, 29 March 2013

❧

Each time life puts the option in front of us to serve inclusively or to take advantage by excluding [others], between washing another's feet or washing our hands of someone else's troubles, let the image of Jesus and the joy of service come to mind.

Homily, 7 August 2005

On Silence

I invite you, men and women of God's word: love silence, search for silence, cultivate silence in your ministry!

Homily, 12 March 2005

On Sin

Feeling like a sinner is one of the most beautiful things that can happen to a person if it leads them to the ultimate consequences [of reconciliation].

El Jesuita, 2010

For me, sin is not a stain that I have to clean. What I should do is ask pardon and make reconciliation, not stop by the cleaner's on my way home.

El Jesuita, 2010

On Soccer as a Metaphor for Life

It's like in soccer: you have to deal with the penalties where they fall; you can't choose where they're going to land. Life is like that, and you have to deal with it even if you don't like it.

Homily, 10 March 2012

On Social Justice

The inclusion or exclusion of the wounded person by the wayside defines all economic, political, social, and religious projects. All of us, each day, are presented with the option of being Good Samaritans or indifferent passersby.

AP Worldstream, 17 April 2005

On Social Media

We try to reach out to people who are far away, via digital means, the web, and brief messaging.

Vatican Insider, 24 February 2012

His first tweet:
Dear friends, I thank you from the heart and I ask you to continue to pray for me. Pope Francis.

Twitter, *@Pontifex*, 17 March 2013

On Spiritual Worldliness

Spiritual worldliness is a form of religious anthropocentrism that has Gnostic elements. Careerism and the search for a promotion come under the category of spiritual worldliness.

America magazine, 13 March 2013

On Statistics

There are those who look with eyes of statistics . . . and most of the time they only see numbers; they only know how to count.

Homily, 12 March 2005

On Suffering

It is from pain and our own limits where we best learn to grow, and from our own flaws surges the deep question: haven't we suffered enough to decide to break old patterns?

Homily, 25 May 2002

Happy are we who, upon hearing the call to justice, feel our insides burn when we see the misery of millions of people in the world.

Homily, 25 May 2006

∽

Suffering is not a virtue in and of itself, but it can be virtuous, depending upon the way in which we deal with it.

El Jesuita, 2010

∽

We are living through serious situations that are dispiriting and frequently take our breath away.

Homily, Ash Wednesday 2004

On Suicide

There was a time when [the Church wouldn't] do funerals for suicides, because [the person] didn't keep walking toward the goal; he put an end to the path when he felt like it. But this is a person who couldn't overcome the contradictions. I don't reject him. I leave it in God's hands.

Sobre el Cielo y la Tierra, 2010

On Tango

I like tango; I danced it when I was young....Tango is something that gives me great pleasure.

El Jesuita, 2010

On Teachers

You [teachers] stand daily before boys and girls who are full of possibilities, desires, fears, and real lack. Children who are demanding, waiting, criticizing, pleading in their own way, [who are] infinitely alone, in need, terrified, [and yet] persistently trusting in you, even if they present a face of indifference, disinterest, or rage. They're alert, waiting to see if you'll offer them something different, or if you'll just close yet another door in their face.

Homily, Easter 2005

❦

Teaching is one of the passionate arts in existence.

Homily, Easter 2008

On Technology

New realities demand new responses.

Annual Message to Educational Communities, Easter 2000

⁓

It's obvious that we can't opt out of being part of the "information society" in which we live, but what we can do is take our time to analyze, to lay out possibilities, to visualize consequences, to exchange points of view, and to listen to other voices.

Homily, Easter 2005

⁓

Technology can help create or disorient. It can re-create things and inform us about reality, thus helping us see the options and decisions before us, or it can, on the contrary, create virtual simulations, illusions, fantasies, and fictions.

Homily, 2002

On Television

Cultural production, especially what's on TV, [is characterized by] programs in which degradation and sexual frivolity, the devaluation of the family, the promotion of vices artificially made up as virtues, and the exaltation of violence are constant.

Letter for the Youth, 1 October 2005

On Time

The things that are truly important require time: to learn a craft or a profession, to know a person and establish an enduring relationship of love or friendship, to know how to distinguish the important from the things we can do without.

Homily, Easter 2005

❧

"Time yields experience," yes, but only if one takes the opportunity to "make experience out of experience."

Homily, Easter 2005

❧

Let me be clear: "take your time" isn't the same as "just let it be."

Homily, Easter 2005

On Truth

Where there is truth, there is also light, but don't confuse light with the flash.

Homily, 4 October 2002

❧

When one is really searching for the truth, one is doing it for good. You don't look for the truth to divide, confront, attack, belittle, or dissolve.

Speech, ADEPA, 6 April 2006

❧

In a society where lies, cover-ups, and hypocrisy have caused people to lose basic trust in the social contract, what could be more revolutionary than the truth?

Annual Message to Educational Communities, 9 April 2003

❧

Only with "the truth will set you free" is it possible to resolve the grave problems of people and nations.

Homily, 25 September 2004

❧

The truth is always combative, but it is also combated.

Homily, 10 April 2002

❧

Truth, goodness, and beauty are inseparable.

Speech, ADEPA, 6 April 2006

❧

It's very hard, in the world of the easy, to believe in the truth.

Homily, 10 April 2002

On Uncertainty

Keep asking why. I can't give you an answer, nor can any bishop, nor the Pope, but [God] will console you.

Homily, 23 March 2012

❧

We are like the Apostles in the Gospel: often we would prefer to hold on to our own security....We are afraid of God's surprises! He always surprises us! The Lord is like that. Dear brothers and sisters, let us not be closed to the newness that God wants to bring into our lives!

Homily, Easter 2013

On Unity

To walk as a people is always slower.

Letter of the Archbishop to the Catechists of Buenos Aires, August 2004

On Vanity

Vanity, showing off, is an attitude that reduces spirituality to a worldly thing, which is the worst sin that could be committed in the Church.

America magazine, 13 March 2013

Look at a peacock. If you look from the front, it's very pretty. But take a few steps back and look at it from behind.... He who falls into self-referential vanity is actually hiding deep misery.

El Mundo, 14 March 2013

On the Vatican and Money

There's always talk about the Vatican's gold, but that's a museum. The Vatican's balance is public, and it's always in deficit; what enters in donations or through museum visits goes to leprosariums, schools, and communities [in need].

Sobre el Cielo y la Tierra, 2010

On the Virgin Mary

Our Lady best transmits to the faithful the joy of God's word, which first filled her with pleasure.

Speech, "The Sunday Homily in Latin America," 19 January 2005

Mary was an expert in listening.

Homily, 7 August 2006

On Vulnerability

Only he who recognizes his vulnerability is capable of unified action.

Homily, 21 August 2003

On Waiting

The capacity to wait is probably one of the most important things we have to learn.

Homily, Easter 2005

On Washing the Feet of AIDS Patients

This gesture is an invitation to the heart of every Christian, because we never lose if we imitate Jesus, if we serve our suffering brothers.

Wall Street Journal, 14 March 2013

On Wealth Inequity

Poor people are persecuted for demanding work, and rich people are applauded for fleeing from justice

BBC News, 14 March 2013

Human rights are not only violated by terrorism, repression, or assassination, but also by unfair economic structures that create huge inequalities.

Guardian, 13 March 2013

On What the Catholic Church
Owes Its Parishioners

Mercy, mercy, mercy.

Bloomberg News, 14 March 2013

On Women

When I was a seminarian, I was dazzled by a girl I met. Her beauty, her intellect surprised me, and well, I walked around dizzy for a good bit. When I returned to the seminary, I couldn't pray for a whole week because this girl always popped into my head. I had to rethink what I was doing. I was still free because I was a seminarian; I could have gone back home, [but] I reaffirmed my decision, the religious path. It would be abnormal if this type of thing didn't happen. When it does happen, one has to resituate oneself.

Sobre el Cielo y la Tierra, 2010

❧

The fact that a woman can't be a priest doesn't mean that she is less than a man.

Sobre el Cielo y la Tierra, 2010

❧

Women's presence in the Church hasn't been emphasized much because the temptation of machismo didn't allow a space to make visible the place of women in the community.

Sobre el Cielo y la Tierra, 2010

On the Word of God

The word of God always offers a choice: convert and ask for help and more light, or close and cling even more tightly to your chains and darkness.

Homily, 13 April 2006

On Work

I thank my father so much for sending me to work [at the age of 13]. Working was one of those things that made me a better person, and, in particular, in the laboratory [where he worked], I learned the good and the bad of all human labor.

El Jesuita, 2010

A person who works should take time to rest, to spend time with family, to enjoy [life], to read, listen to music, play a sport. When work doesn't allow room for healthy leisure time, for restorative rest, then it enslaves [the worker].

El Jesuita, 2010

Man is not made for work; work is made for man.

El Jesuita, 2010

Timeline of Pope Francis's Life

1936

On 17 December, Jorge Mario Bergoglio is born in Flores, Buenos Aires, Argentina, to Mario Jose Bergoglio, an Italian immigrant, and Regina Maria Sivori of Argentina.

1954

Bergoglio graduates from high school with a diploma in chemical technology. He works at a local company for a few years while also studying at a local seminary.

1958

Bergoglio contracts a severe case of pneumonia, and doctors remove part of one lung in order to save his life. He recovers fully.

He decides to devote himself to the priesthood, and on 11 March, he joins the Jesuits as a novice.

1960

Bergoglio receives a degree in philosophy from the Colegio Máximo de San José in Buenos Aires.

1964

Bergoglio begins teaching literature and psychology in Buenos Aires at the Colegio de la Inmaculada and the Colegio del Salvador.

1969

On 13 December, the future Pope is ordained as a priest. He begins work at the Philosophical and Theological Faculty of San Miguel, Argentina, where he becomes a professor of theology and supervises novice priests.

1973

On 22 April, Bergoglio takes his final vows as a Jesuit. In addition to his regular duties, Bergoglio serves as the regional leader in Argentina for the worldwide Jesuit order, a position he will hold for six years.

1980

Bergoglio is appointed Dean at the Philosophical and Theological Faculty of San Miguel. He travels to Germany, where he first views *Mary Untier of Knots*, a painting by Baroque painter Johann Georg Melchior Schmidtner. He is so inspired by the image that he brings a copy back with him to Buenos Aires.

1992

On 27 June, Father Jorge, as he is known, is appointed as Auxiliary Bishop in Buenos Aires.

1998

On 28 February, Bergoglio becomes Archbishop of Buenos Aires.

2001

On 21 February, Pope John Paul II appoints Bergoglio as a Cardinal of the Catholic Church.

2005

Bergoglio begins serving as President of the Argentine Episcopal Conference, a post he will hold until 2011.

It is rumored that Bergoglio came in second when the cardinals met to select a pope after the death of John Paul II. The Conclave instead selected Cardinal Joseph Ratzinger of Germany, who would be elected as Pope Benedict XVI.

2013

On 13 March, Bergoglio is elected as the 266th Pope of the Catholic Church, after two days and five ballots.

Citations

On Age and Aging

Old age, they say...: "Pope Francis to Cardinals," *The Vatican Today*,
15 March 2013, www.news.va/en/news/pope-francis-to-cardinals
-like-good-wine-that-impr.

The old person is the transmitter...: Jorge Bergoglio and Abraham Skorka,
Sobre el Cielo y la Tierra (Buenos Aires: Editorial Sudamericana, 2010).

The bitterness of the old person...: Jorge Bergoglio and Abraham Skorka,
Sobre el Cielo y la Tierra (Buenos Aires: Editorial Sudamericana, 2010).

On Argentina

Is it true...: Jorge Bergoglio and Abraham Skorka, *Sobre el Cielo y la
Tierra* (Buenos Aires: Editorial Sudamericana, 2010).

Our painful political history...: "Mensaje del Sr. Arzobispo en la Misa por la
Educación" (Message from the Archbishop in the Mass for Education),
23 April 2008, www.arzbaires.org.ar/inicio/homilias.html.

Argentina has arrived...: "Mensaje del Arzobispo a las Comunidades Educativas" (Archbishop's Message to Educational Communities), March
2002, www.arzbaires.org.ar/inicio/homilias.html.

I dare to say it...: "Homilía del Sr. Arzobispo en la Misa por la Educación"
(Homily of the Archbishop in the Mass for Education), 6 April 2005,
www.arzbaires.org.ar/inicio/homilias.html.

We live in the most...: "Ponencia del Sr. Arzobispo en la V Conferencia del CELAM" (Speech of the Archbishop in the Fifth Conference of CELAM), 21 May 2007, ncronline.org/news/celam-update-option-poor-alive-and-well-latin-america.

On Argentina's Dirty War

In the Church...: Jorge Bergoglio and Abraham Skorka, *Sobre el Cielo y la Tierra* (Buenos Aires: Editorial Sudamericana, 2010).

We believe that...: Marcela Valente, "Priest's Life Sentence Draws Widespread Praise," Interpress Service, 11 October 2007, www.ipsnews.net/2007/10/rights-argentina-priestrsquos-life-sentence-draws-widespread-praise.

The horrors committed...: Jorge Bergoglio and Abraham Skorka, *Sobre el Cielo y la Tierra* (Buenos Aires: Editorial Sudamericana, 2010).

On Argentina's Leaders

Rather than preventing...: Mark Rice-Oxley, "Pope Francis: The Humble Pontiff with a Practical Approach to Poverty," *Guardian*, 13 March 2013, www.guardian.co.uk/world/2013/mar/13/jorge-mario-bergoglio-pope-poverty.

On Art and Artists

Artists know well...: "Disertación del Sr. Arzobispo en ADEPA" (Archbishop's speech at ADEPA), 6 April 2006, www.arzbaires.org.ar/inicio/homilias.html.

Argentina has given...: "Mensaje del Arzobispo de Buenos Aires a las Comunidades Educativas" (Message of the Archbishop of Buenos Aires to Educational Communities), Easter 2006, www.arzbaires.org.ar/inicio/homilias.html.

The White Crucifixion...: Sergio Rubin and Francesca Ambrogetti, *El Jesuita: Conversaciones con el Cardenal Jorge Bergoglio, S.J.* (Buenos Aires: Vergara, 2010).

On Asking Catholics for Their Prayers

I would like to give you...: Philip Pullella, "New Pope Francis's First
  Words after Election," Reuters, 13 March 2013, www.reuters.com
  /article/2013/03/13/us-pope-succession-text-idUSBRE92C19
  Y20130313.

On Aspirations

No one can grow...: "Homilía del Sr. Arzobispo en el Te Deum del
  25 de Mayo" (Homily of the Archbishop on the May 25 Te Deum),
  25 May 2006, www.arzbaires.org.ar/inicio/homilias.html.

On Assisted Suicide

In Argentina there is...: LifeSiteNews.com, 5 October 2007, www.lifesite
  news.com/news/archive//ldn/2007/oct/07100509.
[Euthanasia is] a culture of discarding...: Speech, Aparecida Document,
  2 October 2007, www.lifenews.com/2013/03/13/new-pope-francis
  -called-abortion-the-death-penalty-for-the-unborn.

On Atheists

I don't say that...: Jorge Bergoglio and Abraham Skorka, *Sobre el Cielo y la
  Tierra* (Buenos Aires: Editorial Sudamericana, 2010).
Not everyone present belongs...: Vatican press conference, 16 March 2013,
  www.news.va/en/news/pope-francis-on-mass-media-and-name.
[I] know more agnostics...: Jorge Bergoglio and Abraham Skorka, *Sobre el
  Cielo y la Tierra* (Buenos Aires: Editorial Sudamericana, 2010).

On Baptizing the Children of Single Parents

The child has absolutely no...: Gianni Valente, "We Are Not Owners of
  the Gifts of the Lord," *30 Giorni*, August 2009, www.30giorni.it
  /articoli_id_21539_l3.htm.
In our ecclesiastical region...: New York Daily News, 14 March 2013,
  www.nydailynews.com/news/world/popebio-article-1.1287994.

On Beauty

Few things are more moving…: "Disertación del Sr. Arzobispo en ADEPA" (Archbishop's speech at ADEPA), 6 April 2006, www.arzbaires.org.ar /inicio/homilias.html.

Because it is human…: "Disertación del Sr. Arzobispo en ADEPA" (Archbishop's speech at ADEPA), 6 April 2006, www.arzbaires.org .ar/inicio/homilias.html.

On Being Chosen as Pope

As you know…: Chelsea J. Carter, Hada Messia, and Richard Allen Greene, "Pope Francis, the Pontiff of Firsts, Breaks with Tradition," CNN, 14 March 2013, www.cnn.com/2013/03/13/world/europe /vatican-pope-selection.

May God forgive you…: Andy Soltis, "Pope Francis Told Cardinals, 'May God Forgive You for What You've Done,'" *New York Post*, 15 March 2013, www.nypost.com/p/news/international/father_forgive_them _7g9eZeF8N5Enl8Y1pQgz4L.

On Being Right…and Wrong

I don't have all the answers…: Sergio Rubin and Francesca Ambrogetti, *El Jesuita: Conversaciones con el Cardenal Jorge Bergoglio, S.J.* (Buenos Aires: Vergara, 2010).

On Birth Control

[Anti-condom zealots want to]…: Jorge Bergoglio and Abraham Skorka, *Sobre el Cielo y la Tierra* (Buenos Aires: Editorial Sudamericana, 2010).

On Bridezilla Weddings

In some churches…: Jorge Bergoglio and Abraham Skorka, *Sobre el Cielo y la Tierra* (Buenos Aires: Editorial Sudamericana, 2010).

On Buenos Aires

Distracted city, dispersed city....: "Homilía del Sr. Arzobispo de Buenos
Aires en Ocasion de la Misa por el Primer Aniversario de la Tragedia
de Cromagnon" (Homily of the Archbishop of Buenos Aires on the Occasion of Mass on the first anniversary of the Cromagnon tragedy),
30 December 2005, www.arzbaires.org.ar/inicio/homilias.html.

For many, Buenos Aires...: Vatican Insider, 15 December 2011, vatican
insider.lastampa.it/en/news/detail/articolo/america-del-sud-south
-america-america-del-sur-10811.

This city does not know....: Homily, 23 March 2012, www.aicaold.com.ar
/docs_blanco.php?id=1888.

At school they taught us...: "Pope Francis — In His Own Words,"
Guardian, 14 March 2013, www.guardian.co.uk/world/2013/mar/14
/new-pope-francis-in-his-own-words.

How lovely it is....: "Homilía del Sr. Arzobispo en la Solemnidad de Corpus Christi" (Homily of the Archbishop on the Solemnity of Corpus
Christi), 24 May 2008, www.arzbaires.org.ar/inicio/homilias.html.

When I pray for....: "Palabras iniciales del Sr. Arzobispo en el Primer Congreso Regional de Pastoral Urbana" (Initial words of the Archbishop
to the First Regional Congress of Urban Parishes), 25 August 2011,
www.arzbaires.org.ar/inicio/homilias.html.

On Cardinals

The cardinalate is a service...: Andrea Tornielli, "Careerism and Vanity:
Sins of the Church," *Vatican Insider,* 24 February 2012, vatican
insider.lastampa.it/en/inquiries-and-interviews/detail/articolo
/america-latina-latin-america-america-latina-12945.

Cardinals are not...: Andrea Tornielli, "Careerism and Vanity: Sins of the
Church," *Vatican Insider,* 24 February 2012, vaticaninsider.lastampa
.it/en/inquiries-and-interviews/detail/articolo/america-latina-latin
-america-america-latina-12945//pag/1/.

On Catechists

I hope that there is…: "Palabras del Sr. Arzobispo al comienzo del Encuentro Arquidiocesano de Catequesis" (Words of the Archbishop at the Start of the Archdiocesan Meeting of Catechists), 12 March 2005, www.arzbaires.org.ar/inicio/homilias.html.

On Catholic Life

When one does not walk…: Homily, first papal Mass, 14 March 2013, chiesa.espresso.repubblica.it/articolo/1350467?eng=y.

To walk, to build…: Homily, First Papal Mass, 14 March 2013, chiesa.espresso.repubblica.it/articolo/1350467?eng=y.

On Celibacy in Priests

Yes, hypothetically, western Catholicism…: Jorge Bergoglio and Abraham Skorka, *Sobre el Cielo y la Tierra* (Buenos Aires: Editorial Sudamericana, 2010).

On Character Flaws

Isn't it fickle…: "Homilía del Sr. Arzobispo en el Te Deum del 25 de Mayo" (Homily of the Archbishop on the May 25 Te Deum), 25 May 2011, www.arzbaires.org.ar/inicio/homilias.html.

It astonished and perplexed…: "Mensaje Cuaresmal del Sr. Arzobispo Jorge Mario Bergoglio S.J. — Miercoles de Ceniza" (Ash Wednesday Message of Archbishop Jorge Mario Bergoglio, S.J.), 22 February 2012, www.arzbaires.org.ar/inicio/homilias.html.

On Child Labor

The promotion and strengthening…: "Carta por la Niñez" (Letter for the Youth), 1 October 2005, www.arzbaires.org.ar/inicio/homilias.html.

On Children

What world are we…: "Disertación de Mons. Jorge Mario Bergoglio en la Sede de la Asociación Cristiana de Empresarios, Sobre el Tema de

Educación" (Dissertation of Monsignor Jorge Mario Bergoglio at the
Headquarters of the Association of Christian Businessmen, on the
Theme of Education), 1 September 1999, www.arzbaires.org.ar/inicio
/homilias.html.

We have, in our hands...: "Homilía del Sr. Arzobispo en la Misa por la
Educación" (Homily of the Archbishop in the Mass for Education),
6 April 2005, www.arzbaires.org.ar/inicio/homilias.html.

We should be cognizant...: "Carta por la Niñez" (Letter for the Youth),
1 October 2005, www.arzbaires.org.ar/inicio/homilias.html.

So many children don't know...: "Mensaje del Arzobispo a los sacerdotes,
religiosos/as y fieles laicos de la Arquidiócesis — Miercoles de Ceniza"
(Archbishop's Message to Priests, Religious People, and Faithful Laity
of the Archdiocese on the Occasion of Ash Wednesday), 25 February
2004, www.arzbaires.org.ar/inicio/homilias.html.

Children are mistreated...: Speech, 2 October 2007, www.lifesitenews.com
/news/archive//ldn/2007/oct/07100509.

On Choices

Each day, we all face...: "Homilía del Sr. Arzobispo en el Te Deum"
(Homily of the Archbishop on the Te Deum), 25 May 2003,
www.arzbaires.org.ar/inicio/homilias.html.

On Choosing the Name Francis

The man of the poor...: "Pope Francis Lays Out Vision of 'Poor Church'
Working for the People," *Guardian*, 16 March 2013, www.guardian
.co.uk/world/2013/mar/16/pope-francis-st-francis-assisi.

Francis is also the man of peace...: Marco della Cava, "Pope Francis
Charms Media in First Media Address," *USA Today*, 16 March 2013,
www.usatoday.com/story/news/world/2013/03/16/pope-francis
-press-conference/1992355.

[Francis of Assisi] brought...: Jorge Bergoglio and Abraham Skorka, *Sobre
el Cielo y la Tierra* (Buenos Aires: Editorial Sudamericana, 2010).

On the Christian Life

The Christian truth is attractive...: "Pope Francis to Cardinals," *The Vatican Today*, 15 March 2013, www.news.va/en/news/pope-francis -to-cardinals-like-good-wine-that-impr.

[Living] the Christian life...: Sergio Rubin and Francesca Ambrogetti, *El Jesuita: Conversaciones con el Cardenal Jorge Bergoglio, S.J.* (Buenos Aires: Vergara, 2010).

The Christian life is always...: "Homilía del Cardenal Bergoglio al Inaugurar El Congreso de Evangelización de la Cultura" (Homily of Cardinal Bergoglio on the Inauguration of the Congress of Cultural Evangelization), 11 March 2006, www.arzbaires.org.ar/inicio/homilias.html.

In the life of every Christian...: "Homilía del Cardenal Bergoglio al Inaugurar El Congreso de Evangelización de la Cultura" (Homily of Cardinal Bergoglio on the Inauguration of the Congress of Cultural Evangelization), 11 March 2006, www.arzbaires.org.ar/inicio /homilias.html.

On Christmas

What is the spirit of Christmas?...: *La Nación*, 23 December 2011.

On the Church

We have to avoid...: Sergio Rubin and Francesca Ambrogetti, *El Jesuita: Conversaciones con el Cardenal Jorge Bergoglio, S.J.* (Buenos Aires: Vergara, 2010).

If, throughout history...: Jorge Bergoglio and Abraham Skorka, *Sobre el Cielo y la Tierra* (Buenos Aires: Editorial Sudamericana, 2010).

The Church is Mother...: "La Homilía Dominical en América Latina — Intervención del Sr. Arzobispo en la Plenaria de la Comisión para América Latina" (The Sunday Homily in Latin America — Presentation by the Archbishop at the Plenary of the Commission for Latin America), 19 January 2005, www.arzbaires.org.ar/inicio/homilias.html.

The Church was, is...: "Homilía del Sr. Cardenal Jorge Mario Bergoglio S.J., al Comenzar la Asamblea del Episcopado" (Homily of Cardinal Jorge Mario Bergoglio S.J., on the Occasion of the Beginning of the Assembly of the Espicopate), 23 April 2007, www.arzbaires.org.ar /inicio/homilias.html.

How I would love a Church...: Nicole Winfield, "Pope Explains Name, Urges 'Church for the Poor,'" *Huffington Post*, 16 March 2013, www.huffingtonpost.com/huff-wires/20130316/eu-vatican-pope.

I must not be scandalized...: Vincent J. Miller, "Quotes from Pope Francis," *America* magazine, 13 March 2013, americamagazine.org /content/all-things/quotes-pope-francis.

On the Church in Buenos Aires

Instead of just being...: Vatican Insider, 24 February 2013, vaticaninsider .lastampa.it/en/inquiries-and-interviews/detail/articolo/america -latina-latin-america-america-latina-12945.

On Church Politics

The Pope [Benedict XVI]...: Andrea Tornielli, "Careerism and Vanity: Sins of the Church," *Vatican Insider*, 24 February 2012, vaticanin sider.lastampa.it/en/inquiries-and-interviews/detail/articolo /america-latina-latin-america-america-latina-12945.

There are sectors within the religions...: Sobre el Cielo y la Tierra, Jorge Bergoglio and Abraham Skorka (Buenos Aires: Editorial Sudameri-cana, 2010).

There have been corrupt periods...: Jorge Bergoglio and Abraham Skorka, *Sobre el Cielo y la Tierra* (Buenos Aires: Editorial Sudamericana, 2010).

On the Church's Emphasis on Suffering

It is true that at one time, [the Church]...: Sergio Rubin and Francesca Ambrogetti, *El Jesuita: Conversaciones con el Cardenal Jorge Bergoglio, S.J.* (Buenos Aires: Vergara, 2010).

On Cities

Every big city...: "Palabras del Sr. Arzobispo al comienzo del Encuentro Arquidiocesano de Catequesis" (Words of the Archbishop at the Start of the Archdiocesan Meeting of Catechists), 12 March 2005, www.arzbaires.org.ar/inicio/homilias.html.

The city is also a mother...: "Homilía del Sr. Arzobispo de Buenos Aires en Ocasión de la Misa por el Primer Aniversario de la Tragedia de Cromagnon" (Homily of the Archbishop of Buenos Aires on the Occasion of Mass on the First Anniversary of the Cromagnon Tragedy), 30 December 2005, www.arzbaires.org.ar/inicio/homilias.html.

On Citizenship

Political society will only endure...: "Dejar la nostalgia y el pesimismo y dar lugar a nuestra sed de encuentro" (Leave behind nostalgia and pessimism and open space to our desire for union), 25 May 1999, www.arzbaires.org.ar/inicio/homilias.html.

We are historical people...: "Mensaje del Arzobispo a las Comunidades Educativas" (Archbishop's Message to Educational Communities), March 2002, www.arzbaires.org.ar/inicio/homilias.html.

We don't have to expect...: "Homilía del Sr. Arzobispo en el Te Deum" (Homily of the Archbishop on the Te Deum), 25 May 2003, www.arzbaires.org.ar/inicio/homilias.html.

People are historical subjects...: "Conferencia del Sr. Arzobispo en la XIII Jornada Arquidiocesana de Pastoral Social" (Archbishop's Speech at the 13th Archdiocesan Social Pastoral Conference), 16 October 2010, www.arzbaires.org.ar/inicio/homilias.html.

On Civilization

It is possible to build...: "Cátedra Juan Pablo II. Congreso sobre la Veritatis Splendor — Disertación de Clausura del Sr. Arzobispo" (Closing Speech of the Archbishop at the John Paul II Veritatis Splendor Congress), 25 September 2004, www.arzbaires.org.ar/inicio/homilias.html.

On the Conclave

The period of the Conclave was full...: "Pope Francis to Cardinals," *The Vatican Today*, 15 March 2013, www.news.va/en/news/pope-francis-to-cardinals-like-good-wine-that-impr.

On Conversation

Would it be possible...: "Mensaje del Arzobispo a las Comunidades Educativas" (Archbishop's Message to Educational Communities), March 2002, www.arzbaires.org.ar/inicio/homilias.html.

In order to have dialogue...: Jorge Bergoglio and Abraham Skorka, *Sobre el Cielo y la Tierra* (Buenos Aires: Editorial Sudamericana, 2010).

True growth in human...: "Mensaje del Arzobispo a las Comunidades Educativas" (Archbishop's Message to Educational Communities), March 2002, www.arzbaires.org.ar/inicio/homilias.html.

On Creativity

The challenge of creative beings...: "Mensaje del Arzobispo a las Comunidades Educativas" (Archbishop's Message to Educational Communities), 9 April 2003, www.arzbaires.org.ar/inicio/homilias.html.

If to build something...: "Mensaje del Arzobispo a las Comunidades Educativas" (Archbishop's Message to Educational Communities), 9 April 2003, www.arzbaires.org.ar/inicio/homilias.htm.

On Death

Death is on my mind every day: Sergio Rubin and Francesca Ambrogetti, *El Jesuita: Conversaciones con el Cardenal Jorge Bergoglio, S.J.* (Buenos Aires: Vergara, 2010).

On the Death of Argentinian President Néstor Kirchner

And we are here today...: "Homilía del Sr. Arzobispo de Buenos Aires Cardenal Jorge Mario Bergoglio S.J. con Motivo de la Misa de

Sufragio del Dr. Néstor Kirchner" (Homily of Archbishop of Buenos Aires, Cardinal Jorge Mario Bergoglio, S.J., during the Mass for Dr. Néstor Kirchner), 27 October 2010, www.arzbaires.org.ar/inicio /homilias.html.

On the Death Penalty

Before, it was one of those…: Jorge Bergoglio and Abraham Skorka, *Sobre el Cielo y la Tierra* (Buenos Aires: Editorial Sudamericana, 2010).

On Democracy

Of course, participating in…: Jorge Bergoglio and Abraham Skorka, *Sobre el Cielo y la Tierra* (Buenos Aires: Editorial Sudamericana, 2010).

On the Devil

Theologically speaking, the Devil…: Jorge Bergoglio and Abraham Skorka, *Sobre el Cielo y la Tierra* (Buenos Aires: Editorial Sudamericana, 2010).

Whoever does not pray…: First homily as Pope, 15 March 2013, www.news.va/en/news/pope-francis-1st-homily-full-text.

In my own experience…: Jorge Bergoglio and Abraham Skorka, *Sobre el Cielo y la Tierra* (Buenos Aires: Editorial Sudamericana, 2010).

On Dignity

There is not a single violation…: "Homilía del Sr. Arzobispo en la Misa por la Educación" (Homily of the Archbishop in the Mass for Education), 18 April 2007, www.arzbaires.org.ar/inicio/homilias.html.

When a person or a people…: "Homilía del Sr. Arzobispo en la Fiesta de San Cayetano" (Homily of the Archbishop on the Feast of Saint Cayetano), 7 August 2007, www.arzbaires.org.ar/inicio/homilias .html.

On Doubt

The greatest leaders...: Jorge Bergoglio and Abraham Skorka, *Sobre el Cielo y la Tierra* (Buenos Aires: Editorial Sudamericana, 2010).

On Drugs

Alcohol and drugs...: "Pope Francis — In His Own Words," *Guardian*, 14 March 2013, www.guardian.co.uk/world/2013/mar/14/new-pope-francis-in-his-own-words.

On Education

Education is the genuine...: "Homilía del Sr. Arzobispo en la Misa por la Educación" (Homily of the Archbishop in the Mass for Education), 27 April 2006, www.arzbaires.org.ar/inicio/homilias.html.

On Elitism

The impatience of the illustrious...: "Homilía del Sr. Arzobispo en el Te Deum" (Homily of the Archbishop on the Te Deum), 25 May 2004, www.arzbaires.org.ar/inicio/homilias.html.

On Evangelism

We have to go out...: "Homilía del Monsignor Jorge Mario Bergoglio, S.J., en el Encuentro Arquidiocesano de Catequesis" (Homily of Monsignor Jorge Mario Bergoglio, S.J., at the Archdiocesan Meeting of Catechists), 11 March 2000, www.arzbaires.org.ar/inicio/homilias.html.

On Exclusivity

Sometimes, I ask myself...: "Palabras del Sr. Arzobispo al Comienzo del Encuentro Arquidiocesano de Catequesis" (Words of the Archbishop at the Start of the Archdiocesan Meeting of Catechists), 12 March 2005, www.arzbaires.org.ar/inicio/homilias.html.

On Faith

People ask why we...: *Washington Post*, 8 August 2003.

Benedict XVI has insisted...: Andrea Tornielli, "Careerism and Vanity: Sins of the Church," *Vatican Insider*, 24 February 2012, vatican insider.lastampa.it/en/inquiries-and-interviews/detail/articolo /america-latina-latin-america-america-latina-12945.

On Family

The family is the natural center...: *Parish and Family*, 18 January 2007.

The Church tries to demonstrate...: *Parish and Family*, 18 January 2007.

Roles of fatherhood, motherhood...: *Parish and Family*, 18 January 2007.

On Foreign Business

Money also has a homeland...: Jorge Bergoglio and Abraham Skorka, *Sobre el Cielo y la Tierra* (Buenos Aires: Editorial Sudamericana, 2010).

On Forgiveness

We ask for the grace...: Homily, 17 March 2013, en.radiovaticana.va/news /2013/03/17/pope_francis:_mass_at_vatican_parish_and_angelus /en1-674221.

If the Lord did not forgive...: Homily, 17 March 2013, www.news.va/en /news/angelus-17-march-2013.

On Fragility

I invite you to recognize...: "Mensaje del Sr. Arzobispo a los Catequistas" (Message from the Archbishop to the Catechists), 21 August 2003, www.arzbaires.org.ar/inicio/homilias.html.

God, when he looks...: "Misa Crismal" (Chrismal Mass), 8 April 2004, www.arzbaires.org.ar/inicio/homilias.html.

On Freedom

The blindness of spirit...: "Homilía del Sr. Arzobispo en el Te Deum" (Homily of the Archbishop on the Te Deum), 25 May 2004, www.arzbaires.org.ar/inicio/homilias.html.

This is the struggle...: "Homilía en la Misa por la Educación" (Homily in the Mass for Education), 4 September 2003, www.arzbaires.org.ar/inicio/homilias.html.

On Giving Money to Beggars

Sometimes I ask someone...: Jorge Bergoglio and Abraham Skorka, *Sobre el Cielo y la Tierra* (Buenos Aires: Editorial Sudamericana, 2010).

On Globalization

To fight the effects...: La Stampa, December 2001.

If we think of globalization...: Jorge Bergoglio and Abraham Skorka, *Sobre el Cielo y la Tierra* (Buenos Aires: Editorial Sudamericana, 2010).

Globalization, as an economic...: "Ponencia del Sr. Arzobispo en la V Conferencia del CELAM" (Speech of the Archbishop in the Fifth Conference of CELAM), 21 May 2007, www.arzbaires.org.ar/inicio/homilias.html.

Globalization as a unidirectional...: Mensaje del Arzobispo a las Comunidades Educativas" (Archbishop's Message to Educational Communities), March 2002, www.arzbaires.org.ar/inicio/homilias.html.

The kind of globalization that...: Jorge Bergoglio and Abraham Skorka, *Sobre el Cielo y la Tierra* (Buenos Aires: Editorial Sudamericana, 2010).

Globalization has signified...: "Ponencia del Sr. Arzobispo en la V Conferencia del CELAM" (Speech of the Archbishop in the Fifth Conference of CELAM), 21 May 2007, www.arzbaires.org.ar/inicio/homilias.html.

From Bangkok to São Paulo...: "Mensaje del Arzobispo a las Comunidades Educativas" (Archbishop's Message to Educational Communities), March 2002, www.arzbaires.org.ar/inicio/homilias.html.

At no other moment...: "Mensaje del Arzobispo a las Comunidades Educativas" (Archbishop's Message to Educational Communities), March 2002, www.arzbaires.org.ar/inicio/homilias.html.

On God

What God cares about most....: "Homilía de la Misa Crismal" (Homily of the Chrismal Mass), 17 April 2003, www.arzbaires.org.ar/inicio/homilias.html.

We can say, without being irreverent...: "Mensaje del Arzobispo a las Comunidades Educativas" (Archbishop's Message to Educational Communities), 21 April 2004, www.arzbaires.org.ar/inicio/homilias.html.

God is not like the idols....: "Homilía del Sr. Arzobispo en la Fiesta de San Cayetano" (Homily of the Archbishop on the Feast of Saint Cayetano), 7 August 2006, www.arzbaires.org.ar/inicio/homilias.html.

If we close the door of our heart...: "Homilía del Sr. Cardenal Jorge Mario Bergoglio con motivo de la celebración de Domingo de Ramos en la Basílica de San José de Flores" (Homily of Cardinal Jorge Mario Bergoglio on the Occasion of the Observance of Ramos Sunday in the Basilica of San Jose de Flores), 15 March 2008, www.arzbaires.org.ar/inicio/homilias.html.

God isn't a kind of Andreani...: Jorge Bergoglio and Abraham Skorka, *Sobre el Cielo y la Tierra* (Buenos Aires: Editorial Sudamericana, 2010).

On God's Gifts

When a man guards his gift...: Jorge Bergoglio and Abraham Skorka, *Sobre el Cielo y la Tierra* (Buenos Aires: Editorial Sudamericana, 2010).

On God's Promises

He doesn't promise riches or power....: "Homilía del Sr. Arzobispo Pronunciada en la Catedral Metropolitana por los Difuntos de la Discoteca al Cumplirse el Primer Mes de los Acontecimientos" (Homily of the Archbishop Given at the Metropolitan Cathedral on the First Month Anniversary of the Discotheque Tragedy), 30 January 2005, www.arzbaires.org.ar/inicio/homilias.html.

On Good Intentions

Intention is not enough...: "Mensaje del Arzobispo a las Comunidades Educativas" (Archbishop's Message to Educational Communities), 21 April 2004, www.arzbaires.org.ar/inicio/homilias.html.

On Gossip

What is gossip?...: Sergio Rubin and Francesca Ambrogetti, *El Jesuita: Conversaciones con el Cardenal Jorge Bergoglio, S.J.* (Buenos Aires: Vergara, 2010).

On Helping the Poor

The great danger....: Jorge Bergoglio and Abraham Skorka, *Sobre el Cielo y la Tierra* (Buenos Aires: Editorial Sudamericana, 2010).

On Himself

And, please, don't stop....: "Homilía del Sr. Arzobispo en la Solemnidad de Corpus Christi" (Homily of the Archbishop on the Solemnity of Corpus Christi), 9 June 2007, www.arzbaires.org.ar/inicio/homilias.html.

I don't like to talk about...: "Homilía del Sr. Arzobispo de Buenos Aires Cardenal Jorge Mario Bergoglio S.J. en el Santuario Ntra. Sra. Madre de los Emigrantes con Motivo de la celebración Eucarística del Día del Migrante" (Homily of the Archbishop of Buenos Aires, Cardinal Jorge Mario Bergoglio, S.J., in the Sanctuary of Our Mother of the Immigrants,

on the Eucharistic Celebration of the Day of the Migrant),
7 September 2008, www.arzbaires.org.ar/inicio/homilias.html.

On His Appointment as Pope

I don't want to keep...: John D. Stoll and Stacey Meichtry, "In Francis'
First Hours, Humility and Pressing Matters," *Wall Street Journal*,
14 March 2013, online.wsj.com/article/SB1000142412788732407770
4578360063416602492.html.

Brothers and sisters...: Philip Pullella, "New Pope Francis's First Words
after Election," Reuters, 13 March 2013, www.reuters.com/article
/2013/03/13/us-pope-succession-text-idUSBRE92C19Y20130313.

And now, let us start this journey...: Philip Pullella, "New Pope Francis's
First Words after Election," Reuters, 13 March 2013, www.reuters.com
/article/2013/03/13/us-pope-succession-text-idUSBRE92C19Y20130313.

On His Family History

[My parents] met in 1934 at Mass...: Sergio Rubin and Francesca Ambrogetti, *El Jesuita: Conversaciones con el Cardenal Jorge Bergoglio, S.J.*
(Buenos Aires: Vergara, 2010).

On His Greatest Fear

It's true that the hedonistic...: Jorge Bergoglio and Abraham Skorka, *Sobre
el Cielo y la Tierra* (Buenos Aires: Editorial Sudamericana, 2010).

On His Humility

I'll stay down here: Chelsea J. Carter, Hada Messia, and Richard Allen
Greene, "Pope Francis, the Pontiff of Firsts, Breaks with Tradition,"
CNN, 14 March 2013, www.cnn.com/2013/03/13/world/europe
/vatican-pope-selection.

I'll just go...: Nicole Winfield, "Argentine Jorge Bergoglio Elected Pope
Francis," Associated Press, 13 March 2013, bigstory.ap.org/article
/cardinals-resume-vote-2nd-day-conclave.

Pray for me: Mandy Fridmann, "Pope Francis Secrets: Journalist Olga
  Wornat Reveals the Catholic Leader's Innermost Thoughts,"
  Huffington Post, 14 March 2013, www.huffingtonpost.com/2013/03/14
  /pope-francis-secrets_n_2875669.html.

On His Mission as Pope

Repair my Church in ruins....: "A Man of Firsts, Pope Francis Is Remark-
  ably Humble and Conservative," *Catholic Online,* 14 March 2013,
  www.catholic.org/hf/faith/story.php?id=50117.

On His Mother's Reaction When He Joined the Priesthood

When I entered seminary....: Sergio Rubin and Francesca Ambrogetti, *El
  Jesuita: Conversaciones con el Cardenal Jorge Bergoglio, S.J.* (Buenos
  Aires: Vergara, 2010).

On Homilies

A good Sunday homily....: "La Homilía Dominical en América Latina —
  Intervención del Sr. Arzobispo en la Plenaria de la Comisión
  para América Latina" (The Sunday Homily in Latin America —
  Presentation by the Archbishop at the Plenary of the Commission
  for Latin America), 19 January 2005, www.arzbaires.org.ar/inicio
  /homilias.html.

The homily is not so much....: "La Homilía Dominical en América Latina
  — Intervención del Sr. Arzobispo en la Plenaria de la Comisión para
  América Latina" (The Sunday Homily in Latin America — Presenta-
  tion by the Archbishop at the Plenary of the Commission for Latin
  America), 19 January 2005, www.arzbaires.org.ar/inicio/homilias.html.

On Homosexuality

The religious ministry sometimes calls attention...: Jorge Bergoglio and
  Abraham Skorka, *Sobre el Cielo y la Tierra* (Buenos Aires: Editorial
  Sudamericana, 2010).

On Hope

Hope is the capacity…: "Mensaje del Arzobispo a las Comunidades Educativas" (Archbishop's Message to Educational Communities), 29 March 2000, www.arzbaires.org.ar/inicio/homilias.html.

Where there is hope…: "Homilía en la Misa por la Educación" (Homily in the Mass for Education), 10 April 2002, www.arzbaires.org.ar /inicio/homilias.html.

On Human Beings

There are two types of men…: "Homilia del Sr. Arzobispo en el Te Deum" (Homily of the Archbishop on the Te Deum), 25 May 2003, www.arzbaires.org.ar/inicio/homilias.html.

On the Human Mystery

There's no guru here…: "Homilía del Sr. Arzobispo de Buenos Aires, Cardenal Jorge Mario Bergoglio S.J. en la Misa en la Catedral Metropolitana, a un mes de la tragedia ferroviaria de Once" (Homily of the Archbishop of Buenos Aires, Cardinal Jorge Mario Bergoglio, S.J., in the Mass at Metropolitan Cathedral, One Month after the Train Tragedy in Once), 23 March 2012, www.arzbaires.org.ar/inicio /homilias.html.

On Human Trafficking and Slavery

No to slavery…: "Homilía del Sr. Arzobispo en Plaza Constitución" (Homily of the Archbishop in Constitution Plaza), 4 September 2009, www.arzbaires.org.ar/inicio/homilias.html.

On Humanity

Every human being…: "Mensaje del Arzobispo a las Comunidades Educativas" (Archbishop's Message to Educational Communities), March 2002, www.arzbaires.org.ar/inicio/homilias.html. ·

We human beings have a complex....: "Mensaje del Arzobispo a las Comunidades Educativas" (Archbishop's Message to Educational Communities), 18 April 2007, www.arzbaires.org.ar/inicio/homilias.html.

On Hypocrites in the Church

We should commit ourselves to....: Speech, Aparecida Document, 2 October 2007.

On Idolatry

The most dangerous idol....: "Intervención del Sr. Arzobispo durante el Servicio de Selijot, en preparación para el Rosh Hashaná, en la Sinagoga de la calle Vidal 2049 de Buenos Aires" (Speech Given by the Archbishop during the Selijot Service, in Preparation for Rosh Hashana, in the 2049 Vidal Street Synagogue of Buenos Aires), 11 September 2004, www.arzbaires.org.ar/inicio/homilias.html.

On Images and Information

When images and information....: "Tercer Congreso de Comunicadores 'Comunicador: ¿Quién es tu prójimo?'" (Third Congress of Communicators: "Communicator: Who Is Your Neighbor?"), 10 October 2002, www.arzbaires.org.ar/inicio/homilias.html.

On Immigrants and Immigration

It seems that nobody here....: "Homilía del Sr. Arzobispo de Buenos Aires Cardenal Jorge Mario Bergoglio S.J. en el Santuario Ntra. Sra. Madre de los Emigrantes con Motivo de la Celebración Eucarística del Día del Migrante" (Homily of the Archbishop of Buenos Aires, Cardinal Jorge Mario Bergoglio, S.J., in the Sanctuary of Our Mother of the Immigrants, on the Eucharistic Celebration of the Day of the Migrant), 7 September 2008, www.arzbaires.org.ar/inicio/homilias.html.

I confess to you....: "Homilía del Sr. Arzobispo de Buenos Aires Cardenal Jorge Mario Bergoglio S.J. en el Santuario Ntra. Sra. Madre de los Emigrantes con Motivo de la Celebración Eucarística del Día del Migrante" (Homily of the Archbishop of Buenos Aires, Cardinal Jorge Mario Bergoglio, S.J., in the Sanctuary of Our Mother of the Immigrants, on the Eucharistic Celebration of the Day of the Migrant), 7 September 2008, www.arzbaires.org.ar/inicio/homilias.html.

On Indifference

Indifference is dangerous...: "Homilía del Sr. Arzobispo en el Te Deum" (Homily of the Archbishop on the Te Deum), 25 May 2003, www.arzbaires.org.ar/inicio/homilias.html.

Those of us who do nothing...: "Homilía del Sr. Arzobispo de Buenos Aires Cardenal Jorge Mario Bergoglio S.J. en el Santuario Ntra. Sra. Madre de los Emigrantes con Motivo de la Celebración Eucarística del Día del Migrante" (Homily of the Archbishop of Buenos Aires, Cardinal Jorge Mario Bergoglio, S.J., in the Sanctuary of Our Mother of the Immigrants, on the Eucharistic Celebration of the Day of the Migrant), 7 September 2008, www.arzbaires.org.ar/inicio/homilias.html.

We do not have the right...: "Homilía del Sr. Arzobispo en el Te Deum" (Homily of the Archbishop on the Te Deum), 25 May 2003, www.arzbaires.org.ar/inicio/homilias.html.

On Inequality

You have to become indignant...: Speech, August 2012, www.abc.es/socie dad/20130314/abci-bergoglio-frases-francisco-201303140850.html.

On Injustice

Perhaps the worst injustice...: "Mensaje del Arzobispo a las Comunidades Educativas" (Archbishop's Message to Educational Communities), 29 March 2000, www.arzbaires.org.ar/inicio/homilias.html.

In the face of grave forms...: "Cátedra Juan Pablo II. Congreso sobre la Veritatis Splendor — Disertación de Clausura del Sr. Arzobispo" (Closing Speech of the Archbishop at the John Paul II Veritatis Splendor Congress), 25 September 2004, www.arzbaires.org.ar/inicio/homilias.html.

It is not enough to avoid injustice...: "Vigilia Pascual" (Easter Vigil), 26 March 2005, www.arzbaires.org.ar/inicio/homilias.html.

On the Jesuits

[I] entered the Jesuit order...: Sergio Rubin and Francesca Ambrogetti, *El Jesuita: Conversaciones con el Cardenal Jorge Bergoglio, S.J.* (Buenos Aires: Vergara, 2010).

On Jesus

Jesus took care...: "Misa Crismal" (Chrismal Mass), 17 April 2003, www.arzbaires.org.ar/inicio/homilias.html.

Jesus does not want us to be still...: "Homilía del Sr. Arzobispo en la Solemnidad de Corpus Christi" (Homily of the Archbishop on the Solemnity of Corpus Christi), 24 May 2008, www.arzbaires.org.ar/inicio/homilias.html.

On Jewish–Catholic Relations

I sincerely hope...: Letter to Rome's Chief Rabbi, Palash R. Ghosh, "Pope Francis: Jews around the World Welcome New Pontiff, Hope for Renewed Catholic-Jewish Cooperation," *International Business Times*, 14 March 2013.

On Latin America

The Church is very conscious...: Speech, 2 October 2007, www.lifesitenews.com/news/archive//ldn/2007/oct/07100509.

Latin America is experiencing…: "Religiosidad Popular como Inculturación de la Fe" (Popular Religiosity as an Inculturation of Faith), 19 January 2008, www.arzbaires.org.ar/inicio/homilias.html.

On Law

From the old "rules of courtesy".…: "Homilía del Sr. Arzobispo en la Misa por la Educación" (Homily of the Archbishop in the Mass for Education), 27 April 2006, www.arzbaires.org.ar/inicio/homilias.html.

On Leadership

Leadership is an art…: "Conferencia del Sr. Arzobispo en la XIII Jornada Arquidiocesana de Pastoral Social" (Archbishop's Speech at the 13th Archdiocesan Social Pastoral Conference), 16 October 2010, www.arzbaires.org.ar/inicio/homilias.html.

Every leader, to become a true leader…: "Conferencia del Sr. Arzobispo en la XIII Jornada Arquidiocesana de Pastoral Social" (Archbishop's Speech at the 13th Archdiocesan Social Pastoral Conference), 16 October 2010, www.arzbaires.org.ar/inicio/homilias.html.

True leadership…: "Conferencia del Sr. Arzobispo en la XIII Jornada Arquidiocesana de Pastoral Social" (Archbishop's Speech at the 13th Archdiocesan Social Pastoral Conference), 16 October 2010, www.arzbaires.org.ar/inicio/homilias.html.

On Life

Life is priceless.…: Homily, 23 March 2012, www.aicaold.com.ar/docs_blanco.php?id=1888.

On Life in the Twenty-First Century

It is the age of "weak thought".…: "Homilía del Sr. Arzobispo en el Te Deum" (Homily of the Archbishop on the Te Deum), 25 May 2004, www.arzbaires.org.ar/inicio/homilias.html.

Curiously, we have more.…: "Homilía del Sr. Arzobispo en el Te Deum"

(Homily of the Archbishop on the Te Deum), 25 May 2004, www.arzbaires.org.ar/inicio/homilias.html.

On Listening

It's not always easy to listen . . . : Jorge Bergoglio, *El Verdadero Poder Es el Servicio* (Buenos Aires: Editorial Claretiana, 2007).

How many problems would . . . : "Homilía del Sr. Arzobispo de Buenos Aires Cardenal Jorge Mario Bergoglio S.J. con Motivo de la XXXIV Peregrinación Juvenil a Pie a Luján" (Homily of the Archbishop of Buenos Aires, Cardinal Jorge Mario Bergoglio, S.J., on the Occasion of the XXXIV Youth Pilgrimage to Lujan), 5 October 2008, www.arzbaires .org.ar/inicio/homilias.html.

Listening is also the capacity . . . : Jorge Bergoglio, *El Verdadero Poder Es el Servicio* (Buenos Aires: Editorial Claretiana, 2007).

On Love

To love is much more than . . . : "Homilía del Sr. Arzobispo en la Misa por la Educación" (Homily of the Archbishop in the Mass for Education), 27 April 2006, www.arzbaires.org.ar/inicio/homilias.html.

But Father, I don't know how to love . . . : "Homilía del Sr. Arzobispo en la Misa por la Educación" (Homily of the Archbishop in the Mass for Education), 21 April 2004, www.arzbaires.org.ar/inicio/homilias.html.

On Lying

Lies and thievery . . . : "Mensaje del Arzobispo a las Comunidades Educativas" (Archbishop's Message to Educational Communities), March 2002, www.arzbaires.org.ar/inicio/homilias.html.

On Marriage

When the husband or the wife gets . . . : Homily, 17 February 2010, www.arzbaires.org.ar/inicio/homilias.html.

On Maturity

It seems to me that a meditation....: "Vigilia Pascual" (Easter Vigil),
26 March 2005, www.arzbaires.org.ar/inicio/homilias.html.

If maturity was only...: "Vigilia Pascual" (Easter Vigil), 26 March 2005,
www.arzbaires.org.ar/inicio/homilias.html.

Maturity implies time: "Vigilia Pascual" (Easter Vigil), 26 March 2005,
www.arzbaires.org.ar/inicio/homilias.html.

On the Media

Be assured that the Church, for her part...: "Address of the Holy Father
Pope Francis," Vatican: The Holy See, 16 March 2013, www.vatican
.va/holy_father/francesco/speeches/2013/march/documents
/papa-francesco_20130316_rappresentanti-media_en.html.

Journalists always present...: "Disertación del Sr. Arzobispo en ADEPA"
(Archbishop's Speech at ADEPA), 6 April 2006, www.arzbaires.org
.ar/inicio/homilias.html.

When the news only...: "Disertación del Sr. Arzobispo en ADEPA"
(Archbishop's Speech at ADEPA), 6 April 2006, www.arzbaires.org
.ar/inicio/homilias.html.

The media can, unfortunately...: "Tercer Congreso de Comunicadores
'Comunicador: ¿Quién es tu prójimo?'" (Third Congress of
Communicators: "Communicator: Who Is Your Neighbor?"),
10 October 2002, www.arzbaires.org.ar/inicio/homilias.html.

The role of the mass media has expanded...: "Address of the Holy Father
Pope Francis," Vatican: The Holy See, 16 March 2013, www.vatican
.va/holy_father/francesco/speeches/2013/march/documents
/papa-francesco_20130316_rappresentanti-media_en.html.

On Mediocrity

Mediocrity is the best drug...: "Homilía del Sr. Arzobispo en el Te
Deum" (Homily of the Archbishop on the Te Deum), 25 May 2004,
www.arzbaires.org.ar/inicio/homilias.html.

On Memory

To make memories...: "Vigilia Pascual" (Easter Vigil), 26 March 2005, www.arzbaires.org.ar/inicio/homilias.html.

The manipulation of memory...: "Vigilia Pascual" (Easter Vigil), 26 March 2005, www.arzbaires.org.ar/inicio/homilias.html.

On Mercy

A little mercy...: Homily, 17 March 2013, www.news.va/en/news /angelus-17-march-2013.

Only someone who has encountered mercy...: John L. Allen Jr., "Profile: New Pope, Jesuit Bergoglio, Was Runner-Up in 2005 Conclave," *National Catholic Reporter*, 3 March 2013, ncronline.org/blogs /ncr-today/papabile-day-men-who-could-be-pope-13.

Mercy is the Lord's most powerful...: Andrea Tornielli, "Mercy. The First Encyclical of Pope Francis," *The Vatican Insider*, 18 March 2013, vaticaninsider.lastampa.it/en/blog-sacri-palazzi-en/detail /articolo/23343.

On the Mistreatment of Children

No one has the right to experiment...: "Homilía del Sr. Arzobispo Pronunciada en la Catedral Metropolitana por los Difuntos de la Discoteca al Cumplirse el Primer Mes de los Acontecimientos" (Homily of the Archbishop Given at the Metropolitan Cathedral on the First Month Anniversary of the Discotheque Tragedy), 30 January 2005, www.arzbaires.org .ar/inicio/homilias.html.

What is happening to our children?...: "Vigilia Pascual" (Easter Vigil), 26 March 2005, www.arzbaires.org.ar/inicio/homilias.html.

On Money

The measure of every...: "Homilía del Sr. Arzobispo en la Misa por la Educación" (Homily of the Archbishop in the Mass for Education), 18 April 2007, www.arzbaires.org.ar/inicio/homilias.html.

On Morals

We speak of morals because . . . : Giacomo Galeazzi, "Cardinal Bergoglio
Defends South America's Christian Roots," V*atican Insider,*
15 December 2011, vaticaninsider.lastampa.it/en/news/detail/articolo
/america-del-sud-south-america-america-del-sur-10811.

On Neoliberalism

The socioeconomic crisis . . . : "Pope Francis — In His Own Words,"
Guardian, 14 March 2013, www.guardian.co.uk/world/2013/mar
/14/new-pope-francis-in-his-own-words.

In the predominant neoliberal culture . . . : "Ponencia del Sr. Arzobispo en la V
Conferencia del CELAM Aparecida 2007" (Speech of the Archbishop
in the Fifth Conference of CELAM), 21 May 2007, www.arzbaires
.org.ar/inicio/homilias.html.

On Parenting

Without these three attitudes . . . : "Homilía del Sr. Arzobispo pronunciada en
la Celebración del Día del Niño por Nacer" (Homily of the Archbishop
Given in Celebration of the Day of the Unborn Child), 25 March 2004,
www.arzbaires.org.ar/inicio/homilias.html.

Only a mother and a father . . . : "Homilía del Sr. Arzobispo en la Fiesta de
San Cayetano" (Homily of the Archbishop on the Feast of Saint Cayetano), 7 August 2007, www.arzbaires.org.ar/inicio/homilias.html.

On Parties and Partying

The party occupies an important place . . . : "Religiosidad Popular como
Inculturación de la Fe" (Popular Religiosity as Inculturation of the
Faith), 19 January 2008, www.arzbaires.org.ar/inicio/homilias.html.

On the Past

What was a sin and injustice . . . : "Homilía del Sr. Arzobispo en la Solemnidad de Corpus Christi" (Homily of the Archbishop on the Solemnity

of Corpus Christi), 9 June 2007, www.arzbaires.org.ar/inicio
/homilias.html.

On Pedophile Priests

The idea that celibacy produces pedophiles...: Jorge Bergoglio and Abraham
Skorka, *Sobre el Cielo y la Tierra* (Buenos Aires: Editorial Sudamericana, 2010).

I think that is the solution...: Jorge Bergoglio and Abraham Skorka, *Sobre
el Cielo y la Tierra* (Buenos Aires: Editorial Sudamericana, 2010).

On Pessimism

Let us never yield to pessimism...: "Pope Francis to Cardinals," *The Vatican
Today,* 15 March 2013, www.news.va/en/news/pope-francis-to
-cardinals-like-good-wine-that-impr.

On Politics

Politics is a noble activity...: "Pope Francis: From Abortion to the Falk-
lands," *Telegraph,* 13 March 2013, www.telegraph.co.uk/news/religion
/the-pope/9928854/Pope-Francis-from-abortion-to-the-Falklands
-the-new-pontiffs-top-quotes.html.

It's true that I, like my entire family...: Sergio Rubin and Francesca
Ambrogetti, *El Jesuita: Conversaciones con el Cardenal Jorge Bergoglio,
S.J.* (Buenos Aires: Vergara, 2010).

On Politicians

Sometimes they have to put out a fire...: "Jornadas Arquidiocesanas de
Pastoral Social" (Archdiocese Social Pastoral Conference), 2001,
www.arzbaires.org.ar/inicio/homilias.html.

Some people say to me...: "Homilía del Sr. Arzobispo en la Fiesta de San
Cayetano" (Homily of the Archbishop on the Feast of Saint Cayetano),
7 August 2008, www.arzbaires.org.ar/inicio/homilias.html.

On Pope Benedict XVI

I think with great affection...: "Pope Francis to Cardinals," *The Vatican Today*, 15 March 2013, www.news.va/en/news/pope-francis-to -cardinals-like-good-wine-that-impr.

It was [God] who inspired the decision...: "Pope Francis on Mass Media and Name," *The Vatican Today*, 16 March 2013, www.news.va/en/news /pope-francis-on-mass-media-and-name.

On Possibilities

Human history, our history...: "Mensaje del Arzobispo a las Comunidades Educativas" (Archbishop's Message to Educational Communities), 9 April 2003, www.arzbaires.org.ar/inicio/homilias.html.

On Poverty

A community that stops kneeling...: "Mensaje del Arzobispo a las Comunidades Educativas" (Archbishop's Message to Educational Communities), March 2002, www.arzbaires.org.ar/inicio/homilias.html.

Is there anything more humiliating than...: "Mensaje del Arzobispo a las Comunidades Educativas" (Archbishop's Message to Educational Communities), March 2002, www.arzbaires.org.ar/inicio/homilias .html.

On Power

If the most powerful used...: "Homilía del Sr. Arzobispo en la Fiesta de San Cayetano" (Homily of the Archbishop on the Feast of Saint Cayetano), 7 August 2005, www.arzbaires.org.ar/inicio/homilias.html.

He who has a little more power...: "Homilía del Sr. Arzobispo en la Fiesta de San Cayetano" (Homily of the Archbishop on the Feast of Saint Cayetano), 7 August 2005, www.arzbaires.org.ar/inicio /homilias.html.

On Prayer

Let us always pray for us…: "New Pope Francis's Words after Election," Reuters, 13 March 2013, www.reuters.com/article/2013/03/13/us -pope-succession-text-idUSBRE92C19Y20130313.

On the Priesthood

To be an open priest…: "Carta a los sacerdotes de la Arquidiócesis" (Letter to the Priests of the Archdiocese), 1 October 1999, www.arzbaires.org .ar/inicio/homilias.html.

As pastors, it behooves…: "La Homilía Dominical en América Latina — Intervención del Sr. Arzobispo en la Plenaria de la Comisión para América Latina" (The Sunday Homily in Latin America — Presentation by the Archbishop at the Plenary of the Commission for Latin America), 19 January 2005, www.arzbaires.org.ar/inicio/homilias.html.

On Priests Who Stray

If one of them comes to me…: Jorge Bergoglio and Abraham Skorka, *Sobre el Cielo y la Tierra* (Buenos Aires: Editorial Sudamericana, 2010).

The double life doesn't do anyone good…: Jorge Bergoglio and Abraham Skorka, *Sobre el Cielo y la Tierra* (Buenos Aires: Editorial Sudamericana, 2010).

On Prison Visits

It's horrific for me to go to a jail…: Jorge Bergoglio and Abraham Skorka, *Sobre el Cielo y la Tierra* (Buenos Aires: Editorial Sudamericana, 2010).

On Public Transportation

I almost always take [the subway]…. Sergio Rubin and Francesca Ambrogetti, *El Jesuita: Conversaciones con el Cardenal Jorge Bergoglio, S.J.* (Buenos Aires: Vergara, 2010).

On the Relationship between Church and State

It isn't bad if religion dialogues...: Jorge Bergoglio and Abraham Skorka, *Sobre el Cielo y la Tierra* (Buenos Aires: Editorial Sudamericana, 2010).

On Relativism

The modern city is relativist...: "Palabras iniciales del Sr. Arzobispo en el Primer Congreso Regional de Pastoral Urbana" (Initial words of the Archbishop to the First Regional Congress of Urban Parishes), 25 August 2011, www.arzbaires.org.ar/inicio/homilias.html.

On Religious Diversity

The massive migratory movements...: "Cátedra Juan Pablo II. Congreso sobre la Veritatis Splendor — Disertación de Clausura del Sr. Arzobispo" (Closing Speech of the Archbishop at the John Paul II Veritatis Splendor Congress), 25 September 2004, www.arzbaires.org.ar/inicio /homilias.html.

To recognize, accept, and live with all...: "Homilía del Sr. Arzobispo en la Misa por la Educación" (Homily of the Archbishop in the Mass for Education), 27 April 2006, www.arzbaires.org.ar/inicio/homilias.html.

On Religious Experiences

That is the religious experience...: Sergio Rubin and Francesca Ambrogetti, *El Jesuita: Conversaciones con el Cardenal Jorge Bergoglio, S.J.* (Buenos Aires: Vergara, 2010).

On Religious Life

When we walk without the cross...: Homily, first papal Mass, 14 March 2013, chiesa.espresso.repubblica.it/articolo/1350467?eng=y.

Often, we feel fatigued and tired...: "Mensaje del Arzobispo a los sacerdotes, religiosos/as y fieles laicos de la Arquidiócesis — Miercoles de Ceniza" (Archbishop's Message to Priests, Religious People, and

Faithful Laity of the Archdiocese on the Occasion of Ash Wednesday), 25 February 2004, www.arzbaires.org.ar/inicio/homilias.html.

Jesus did not preach His own politics...: Gianni Valente, "That Neo-clericalism Which 'Hijacks' the Sacraments," *Vatican Insider*, 5 September 2012, vaticaninsider.lastampa.it/en/inquiries-and-interviews/detail/articolo/sacramenti-sacramentos-the-sacraments-17899.

On Religious Vocations

The religious vocation...: Sergio Rubin and Francesca Ambrogetti, *El Jesuita: Conversaciones con el Cardenal Jorge Bergoglio, S.J.* (Buenos Aires: Vergara, 2010).

The Church is in great need...: "Cátedra Juan Pablo II. Congreso sobre la Veritatis Splendor — Disertación de Clausura del Sr. Arzobispo" (Closing Speech of the Archbishop at the John Paul II Veritatis Splendor Congress), 25 September 2004, www.arzbaires.org.ar/inicio/homilias.html.

Jesus teaches us another way...: Douglas Feiden, "Pope Francis, the New Leader of the Catholic Church," *New York Daily News*, 14 March 2013, www.nydailynews.com/news/world/popebio-article-1.1287994.

On Responsibility

We must stop hiding the pain...: "Homilía del Sr. Arzobispo en el Te Deum" (Homily of the Archbishop on the Te Deum), 25 May 2003, www.arzbaires.org.ar/inicio/homilias.html.

On the Role of Pope

Christ is the Church's pastor...: "Address of the Holy Father Pope Francis," Vatican: The Holy See, 16 March 2013, www.vatican.va/holy_father/francesco/speeches/2013/march/documents/papa-francesco_20130316_rappresentanti-media_en.html.

On the Roman Curia

I see it as a body that gives service...: Andrea Tornielli, "Careerism and
Vanity: Sins of the Church," *Vatican Insider*, 24 February 2012, vatican
insider.lastampa.it/en/inquiries-and-interviews/detail/articolo
/america-latina-latin-america-america-latina-12945.

On Rome

I hope that this journey of the Church...: "New Pope Francis's Words after
-Election," Reuters, 13 March 2013, www.reuters.com/article
/2013/03/13/us-pope-succession-text-idUSBRE92C19Y20130313.

On Salvation

There is no middle ground...: "Mensaje del Sr. Arzobispo en la Misa de
Noche Buena" (Message from the Archbishop during Christmas Eve
Mass), 25 December 2003, www.arzbaires.org.ar/inicio/homilias.html.

On Scandals in the Church

Look at the Church, holy and sinful...: Andrea Tornielli, "Careerism
and Vanity: Sins of the Church," *Vatican Insider*, 24 February 2012,
vaticaninsider.lastampa.it/en/inquiries-and-interviews/detail
/articolo/america-latina-latin-america-america-latina-12945.

On Schools

Our schools should be a space...: "Mensaje del Arzobispo a las Comuni-
dades Educativas" (Archbishop's Message to Educational Communi-
ties), 9 April 2003, www.arzbaires.org.ar/inicio/homilias.html.
The essential function of the school...: "Carta por la Niñez" (Letter for the
Youth), 1 October 2005, www.arzbaires.org.ar/inicio/homilias.html.
If our schools are not a space...: "Mensaje del Arzobispo a las Comunidades
Educativas" (Archbishop's Message to Educational Communities),
21 April 2004, www.arzbaires.org.ar/inicio/homilias.html.

On Sectarianism

Sectarian attitudes in the social...: "Pope Francis — In His Own Words,"
Guardian, 14 March 2013, www.guardian.co.uk/world/2013/mar/14
/new-pope-francis-in-his-own-words.

On Self-Sufficiency

When someone is self-sufficient...: Jorge Bergoglio and Abraham Skorka,
Sobre el Cielo y la Tierra (Buenos Aires: Editorial Sudamericana, 2010).

On Service

Service is the rejection of indifference...: "Homilía pronunciada por S.E.R.
Mons. Jorge Mario Bergoglio en el Te Deum" (Homily given by
SER Monsignor Jorge Mario Bergoglio for the Te Deum), 25 May
2001, www.arzbaires.org.ar/inicio/homilias.html.

Power is service...: "Homilía del Sr. Arzobispo en la Fiesta de San
Cayetano" (Homily of the Archbishop on the Feast of Saint Cayetano),
7 August 2005, www.arzbaires.org.ar/inicio/homilias.html.

The person who is most high among us...: Carol Glatz, "Pope Washes Feet
of 12 Young Detainees to Serve Them 'from the Heart,'" *National
Catholic Reporter*, 28 March 2013, ncronline.org/news/vatican/pope
-washes-feet-12-young-detainees-serve-them-heart.

Each time life puts the option...: "Homilía del Sr. Arzobispo en la Fiesta de
San Cayetano" (Homily of the Archbishop on the Feast of Saint Cayetano), 7 August 2005, www.arzbaires.org.ar/inicio/homilias.html.

On Silence

I invite you, men and women...: "Palabras del Sr. Arzobispo al comienzo
del Encuentro Arquidiocesano de Catequesis" (Words of the Archbishop at the Start of the Archdiocesan Meeting of Catechists),
12 March 2005, www.arzbaires.org.ar/inicio/homilias.html.

On Sin

Feeling like a sinner...: Sergio Rubin and Francesca Ambrogetti, *El Jesuita: Conversaciones con el Cardenal Jorge Bergoglio, S.J.* (Buenos Aires: Vergara, 2010).

For me, sin is not a stain...: Sergio Rubin and Francesca Ambrogetti, *El Jesuita: Conversaciones con el Cardenal Jorge Bergoglio, S.J.* (Buenos Aires: Vergara, 2010).

On Soccer as a Metaphor for Life

It's like in soccer...: "Homilía del Sr. Cardenal en el Encuentro Arquidiocesano de Catequistas 2012" (Homily of the Cardinal at the 2012 Archdiocesan Meeting of Catechists), 10 March 2012, www.arzbaires .org.ar/inicio/homilias.html.

On Social Justice

The inclusion or exclusion...: "In Their Own Words: Key Cardinals on Important Issues," *AP Worldstream*, 17 April 2005.

On Social Media

We try to reach out to people...: Andrea Tornielli, "Careerism and Vanity: Sins of the Church," *Vatican Insider*, 24 February 2012, vatican insider.lastampa.it/en/inquiries-and-interviews/detail/articolo /america-latina-latin-america-america-latina-12945.

Dear friends, I thank you...: Twitter, @Pontifex, 17 March 2013.

On Spiritual Worldliness

Spiritual worldliness is...: Vincent J. Miller, "Quotes from Pope Francis," *America* magazine, 13 March 2013, americamagazine.org/content /all-things/quotes-pope-francis.

On Statistics

There are those who look . . . : "Palabras del Sr. Arzobispo al comienzo del
Encuentro Arquidiocesano de Catequesis" (Words of the Archbishop
at the Start of the Archdiocesan Meeting of Catechists), 12 March 2005,
www.arzbaires.org.ar/inicio/homilias.html.

On Suffering

It is from pain and our own limits . . . : "Homilía pronunciada por el Sr. Arzobispo en el Te Deum" (Homily Given for the Te Deum), 25 May 2002,
www.arzbaires.org.ar/inicio/homilias.html.

Happy are we who . . . : "Homilía pronunciada por el Sr. Arzobispo en
el Te Deum" (Homily Given for the Te Deum), 25 May 2006,
www.arzbaires.org.ar/inicio/homilias.html.

Suffering is not a virtue in . . . : Sergio Rubin and Francesca Ambrogetti,
El Jesuita: Conversaciones con el Cardenal Jorge Bergoglio, S.J. (Buenos
Aires: Vergara, 2010).

We are living through serious situations . . . : "Mensaje del Arzobispo a los
sacerdotes, religiosos/as y fieles laicos de la Arquidiócesis — Miercoles
de Ceniza" (Archbishop's Message to Priests, Religious People, and
Faithful Laity of the Archdiocese on the Occasion of Ash Wednesday),
25 February 2004, www.arzbaires.org.ar/inicio/homilias.html.

On Suicide

There was a time when [the Church wouldn't] . . . : Jorge Bergoglio and
Abraham Skorka, *Sobre el Cielo y la Tierra* (Buenos Aires: Editorial
Sudamericana, 2010).

On Tango

I like tango; I danced it . . . : Sergio Rubin and Francesca Ambrogetti, *El
Jesuita: Conversaciones con el Cardenal Jorge Bergoglio, S.J.* (Buenos
Aires: Vergara, 2010).

On Teachers

You [teachers] stand daily before...: "Homilía del Sr. Arzobispo en la Misa por la Educación" (Homily of the Archbishop in the Mass for Education), 6 April 2005, www.arzbaires.org.ar/inicio/homilias.html.

Teaching is one of the passionate...: "Homilía del Sr. Arzobispo en la Misa por la Educación" (Homily of the Archbishop in the Mass for Education), 23 April 2008, www.arzbaires.org.ar/inicio/homilias.html.

On Technology

New realities demand new responses...: "Mensaje del Arzobispo a las Comunidades Educativas" (Archbishop's Message to Educational Communities), 29 March 2000, www.arzbaires.org.ar/inicio/homilias.html.

It's obvious that we can't opt out...: "Homilía del Sr. Arzobispo en la Misa por la Educación" (Homily of the Archbishop in the Mass for Education), 6 April 2005, www.arzbaires.org.ar/inicio/homilias.html.

Technology can help create or disorient...: Homily, 2002, www.arzbaires.org .ar/inicio/homilias.html.

On Television

Cultural production, especially...: "Carta por la Niñez" (Letter for the Youth), 1 October 2005, www.arzbaires.org.ar/inicio/homilias.html.

On Time

The things that are truly important...: "Vigilia Pascual" (Easter Vigil), 26 March 2005, www.arzbaires.org.ar/inicio/homilias.html.

"Time yields experience," yes...: "Vigilia Pascual" (Easter Vigil), 26 March 2005, www.arzbaires.org.ar/inicio/homilias.html.

Let me be clear...: "Vigilia Pascual" (Easter Vigil), 26 March 2005, www.arzbaires.org.ar/inicio/homilias.html.

On Truth

Where there is truth...: Homily, 4 October 2002, www.arzbaires.org.ar /inicio/homilias.html.

When one is really searching for the truth...: "Disertación del Sr. Arzobispo

On Uncertainty

On Unity

On Vanity

Vanity, showing off....: Vincent J. Miller, "Quotes from Pope Francis," *America* magazine, 13 March 2013, americamagazine.org/content /all-things/quotes-pope-francis.

Look at a peacock...: Irene Hernandez Velsaco, "Bergoglio: 'Los males de la iglesia se llaman vanidad y arribismo,'" *El Mundo*, 14 March 2013, www.elmundo.es/elmundo/2013/03/14/internacional/1363255333. html.

On the Vatican and Money

There's always talk about the Vatican's gold...: Jorge Bergoglio and Abraham Skorka, *Sobre el Cielo y la Tierra* (Buenos Aires: Editorial Sudamericana, 2010).

On the Virgin Mary

Our Lady best transmits to the faithful...: "La Homilía Dominical en América Latina — Intervención del Sr. Arzobispo en la Plenaria de la Comisión para América Latina" (The Sunday Homily in Latin America — Presentation by the Archbishop at the Plenary of the Commission for Latin America), 19 January 2005, www.arzbaires.org.ar/inicio /homilias.html.

Mary was an expert in listening: "Homilía del Sr. Arzobispo en la Fiesta de San Cayetano" (Homily of the Archbishop on the Feast of Saint Cayetano), 7 August 2006, www.arzbaires.org.ar/inicio/homilias .html.

On Vulnerability

Only he who recognizes his vulnerability...: "Mensaje del Sr. Arzobispo a los Catequistas" (Archbishop's Message to Catechists), 21 August 2003, www.arzbaires.org.ar/inicio/homilias.html.

On Waiting

The capacity to wait....: "Vigilia Pascual" (Easter Vigil), 26 March 2005, www.arzbaires.org.ar/inicio/homilias.html.

On Washing the Feet of AIDS Patients

This gesture is an invitation....: John Lyons, Ken Parks, and Matthew Cowley, " 'Father Jorge' Rose from Modest Roots," *Wall Street Journal*, 14 March 2013, online.wsj.com/article/SB1000142412788732407770 4578358582371775780.html.

On Wealth Inequity

Poor people are persecuted...: "Pope Francis: Life in Pictures and Quotes," BBC News, 14 March 2013, www.bbc.co.uk/news/world-21775333.
Human rights are not...: Mark Rice-Oxley, "Pope Francis: The Humble Pontiff with Practical Approach to Poverty," *Guardian*, 13 March 2013, www.guardian.co.uk/world/2013/mar/13 /jorge-mario-bergoglio-pope-poverty.

On What the Catholic Church Owes Its Parishioners

Mercy, mercy, mercy: Jeffrey Donovan, "Francis Ventures Out of Vatican on First Day as Pope," Bloomberg News, 14 March 2013, www.bloom berg.com/news/2013-03-13/argentina-s-cardinal-jorge-bergoglio-is -elected-pope-francis-i.html.

On Women

When I was a seminarian....: Jorge Bergoglio and Abraham Skorka, *Sobre el Cielo y la Tierra* (Buenos Aires: Editorial Sudamericana, 2010).
The fact that a woman....: Jorge Bergoglio and Abraham Skorka, *Sobre el Cielo y la Tierra* (Buenos Aires: Editorial Sudamericana, 2010).
Women's presence in the Church...: Jorge Bergoglio and Abraham Skorka, *Sobre el Cielo y la Tierra* (Buenos Aires: Editorial Sudamericana, 2010).

On the Word of God

The word of God always offers a choice...: "Misa Crismal" (Chrismal Mass), 13 April 2006, www.arzbaires.org.ar/inicio/homilias.html.

On Work

I thank my father...: Sergio Rubin and Francesca Ambrogetti, *El Jesuita: Conversaciones con el Cardenal Jorge Bergoglio, S.J.* (Buenos Aires: Vergara, 2010).

A person who works should take time to rest...: Sergio Rubin and Francesca Ambrogetti, *El Jesuita: Conversaciones con el Cardenal Jorge Bergoglio, S.J.* (Buenos Aires: Vergara, 2010).

Man is not made for work...: Sergio Rubin and Francesca Ambrogetti, *El Jesuita: Conversaciones con el Cardenal Jorge Bergoglio, S.J.* (Buenos Aires: Vergara, 2010).

About the Editors

JULIE SCHWIETERT COLLAZO has written for a variety of magazines, including *Time*, *National Geographic Traveler*, and *Latina*, reporting widely on Latin America. She lives in New York, though she has called San Juan, Puerto Rico, and Mexico City home as well. Her blog is www.collazo projects.com.

LISA ROGAK is the *New York Times* bestselling author of more than forty books and hundreds of newspaper and magazine articles. Her books have been published in more than two dozen languages. She lives in New Hampshire. Her website is www.lisarogak.com.